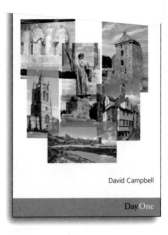

David Campbell

Day One

Series Editor: Brian H Edwards

Day One

John **Knox**

75

Victory!

Riots, siege, and civil war followed Knox's return to Scotland and for a time, the future of the reforming movement hung in the balance. But with history-making help from English troops the longed-for victory was finally achieved

Two months before Knox arrived in Scotland in 1559 a proclamation had been made at the market cross in Edinburgh by order of the Queen-Regent, Mary of Lorraine: no person was to preach or administer the sacraments without authority from the bishops. Throughout the previous year, the Queen-Regent had been surprisingly friendly toward the leading reformers. She had listened to their petitions for the reformation of religion and for protection from hostile clergy, and had given them various assurances. Some were so taken in by such expressions of goodwill that they even went so far as to rebuke those who "appeared to suspect in her any venom of hypocrisy". In the event, however, it was the ones who suspected a "venom of hypocrisy" who were proved right. Mary had needed the support of the Protestant nobles for certain measures that she wished to carry through Parliament and she could not afford to antagonise them. However, as soon as she had achieved her goal, the mask was dropped and the Protestants saw her for the enemy of reformation

Above: St Andrews Castle

Facing page: Church of the Holy Rude, St John Street, Stirling

40

BERWICK

RIVER TWEED

NORHAM

BERWICK-UPON-TWEED

1 BERWICK PARISH CHURCH
2 WALLACE GREEN CHURCH OF SCOTLAND
3 BERWICK CASTLE
4 BERWICK TRAIN STATION AND BUS STATION
5 TOWN CENTRE PARKING WITH PUBLIC TOILETS
6 TOURIST INFORMATION CENTRE, MARYGATE

41

Left: King Edward VI (1537–53)

he would have been in serious trouble.

When the offer of the bishopric of Rochester had been made to Knox, he had refused it. In February 1553 another position was offered to him: the rectorship of All-Hallows in Bread Street, London. But he declined this as well. The reformation of the Church of England had not gone far enough for him to accept a permanent charge in good conscience. In Berwick and Newcastle he seems to have been given considerable freedom to preach and to administer the Lord's Supper as he thought right. Instead of using bread that was "unleavened and round", as the 1549 Prayer Book

instructed, Knox used common bread. Again, instead of kneeling to receive the bread and wine, the people sat. If he were to accept a bishopric or a rectorship, however, it would mean a level of conformity to the Church's beliefs and practices that was impossible for him.

Death of the King
On 6 July 1553, King Edward VI died at the age of sixteen. 'We had' said Knox, 'a king of so godly disposition towards virtue and the truth of God, that none from the beginning passed him, and to my knowledge, none of his years did ever match him.' His sister Mary was proclaimed queen on 19 July.

CONTENTS

● Meet John Knox **5**

❶ 'One is sufficient for a sacrifice' **7**

❷ Striking at the root **23**

❸ 'That great rest' **33**

❹ Travels, trials, and triumphs **49**

❺ City of refuge **63**

❻ Victory! **75**

❼ A fearless preacher **91**

❽ The final years **103**

● Useful information for travellers **117**

● Bibliography **121**

● Monarchs and Regents **121**

● A summary of Knox's life **122**

● Also in this series **124**

© Day One Publications 2003 First printed 2003

All Scripture quotations are taken from the Authorized Version

A Catalogue record is held at The British Library   ISBN 1 903087 34 1

Published by Day One Publications P O Box 66, Leominster, HR6 0XB

☎ 01568 613 740 FAX 01568 611 473 email—sales@dayone.co.uk www.dayone.co.uk   All rights reserved

Design: Steve Devane Printed by Alderson Brothers, Molesey, Surrey

Meet John Knox

Besieged in the castle of St Andrews, chained for nineteen months to the oar of a French galley, forced to flee the country for safety, burned in effigy on the streets of Edinburgh, summoned again and again to appear before Mary, Queen of Scots, shot at in his own home, preaching week by week to thousands—Knox's life was full of colour and drama. He lived at a time in English and Scottish history when it was often very costly to be a Christian. His friend and mentor, George Wishart, was burnt at the stake for the truths he preached. Knox himself was frequently in danger of his life for he had many powerful enemies. But with great boldness he carried on the work he had been called by God to do—with remarkable results.

The impact of John Knox on 16th century Scotland was immense, particularly in connection with the reformation of the church. His courage, vision, preaching and writing, and his perseverance in the face of all difficulties and dangers enabled him to win immense benefits for his fellow countrymen and significantly moulded the later history and culture of Scotland. John Knox is unquestionably one of the greatest figures in Scottish history; a man who deserves to be remembered.

Facing page: *Statue of Knox in the courtyard of New College*

① 'One is sufficient for a sacrifice'

John Knox began his life's work as a preacher and reformer in the Scottish town of St Andrews. A corrupt church, a murdered cardinal, a besieged castle, and a personal experience of persecution form the background to that beginning

In the long history of Scottish Christianity, the year 1560 towers in significance above most. For decades vehement and violent resistance had been offered to those who were endeavouring to reform the church. Many suffered martyrdom; others had to flee the country. At times it seemed that their efforts would end in defeat. But by the blessing of God progress continued to be made until, in August 1560, a series of acts were passed by the Scottish Parliament that brought the most far reaching of changes. The authority of the Pope throughout Scotland was abolished, the celebration of the mass was prohibited, a Confession of Faith that gave expression to key biblical truths was adopted, and every act that had been passed in opposition to the reforming movement was repealed. The way had been opened for a church to be formed that in doctrine, worship, and practice far more faithfully reflected the teachings of the Bible. In the story of how all this came about, no name stands out more prominently than that of John Knox.

Above: John Knox from an old engraving

Facing page: St Andrew's Castle, the scene of George Wishart's martyrdom. The letters 'GW' on the road in front of the tower mark the actual spot where Wishart was martyred (not shown in this picture)

Martin Luther

Martin Luther was born in Eisleben in Germany on 10 November 1483. Anxiety about his spiritual state led him to become a monk in 1505, but it was not until several years later, through coming to an understanding of the doctrine of justification by faith alone, that he found peace with God. He first came into conflict with the Roman Catholic Church in 1517 when he publicly opposed the sale of indulgences, a means of obtaining spiritual privileges—such as the pardon of sin—through the payment of a sum of money. This initial conflict led ultimately to a complete break with Roman Catholicism and to a determined opposition to it for the rest of his life. In September1522, his translation of the New Testament into German was printed and copies of it were smuggled into England and Scotland. Luther was a fearless debater, powerful preacher and prolific writer. He died on 18 February 1546.

It will set the scene for Knox's life and work if we glance at the urgent need that there was for the Scottish church to be reformed. Among the bishops, abbots, friars, and canons in the church, there was appalling ignorance. A contemporary of Knox tells us that many believed the New Testament to be a book written by the German reformer Martin Luther. Laws were passed prohibiting it from being read and when one reformer was on trial and pulled a New Testament from his sleeve, the cry went up: 'Behold, he has the book of heresy in his sleeve, which makes all the confusion in the Kirk!' Many of the clergy were almost illiterate.

Ignorance, however, was far from being the church's only problem. In spite of a profession of chastity on the part of each clergyman, there was rampant immorality. Cardinal David Beaton, Archbishop of St Andrews, for example, is reckoned to have been the father of up to twenty illegitimate children. But it was not only the higher clergy who behaved in this way. Ordinary priests were notoriously immoral as well.

Another problem was greed. More than half of Scotland's wealth was in the hands of the church and the priests seemed determined to grasp as much of

Left: Sketch of Hamilton parting from his friends at the stake

Facing page: George Wishart (top) and Patrick Hamilton

the remaining half as they could. Tithes were rigorously exacted during the course of people's lives and when they were dying, every effort was made to extract from them a bequest.

The church was equally corrupt in doctrine. People were taught that subjection to the Pope was essential to their salvation; that forgiveness of sins for both the living and the dead could be obtained through the sacrifice of the mass; that a reduction of the time spent in purgatory was something that could be purchased; and that the Virgin Mary and the departed saints were mediators between themselves and God in addition to the Lord Jesus. As a consequence there was no insistence of faith in Jesus as the only way to be right with God. People were conditioned to rely on priests, on penance, and on papal pardons for their entrance into heaven. Had there been access to

the Scriptures in a language that was understood, the fallacy of these errors would have been exposed. But the Scriptures were in Latin—which few could read— and the people were forbidden to read the Bible anyway. Under such circumstances it is hardly surprising that there was almost universal ignorance of the gospel.

The need for reform then, was glaring, and to some extent the church's leaders recognized this. But there was an extreme reluctance to make anything other than the most superficial of changes, whilst to those who pressed for thorough reform, especially in the realm of doctrine, the most violent opposition was raised. Between 1528 and 1560 about twenty people who demanded reform were burnt at the stake. Others were imprisoned or heavily fined. Many, in order to escape the persecution, either took refuge in England where they were

Above: St Salvator's Chapel, North Street, Haddington, where Knox's St Andrews' pulpit now stands

marginally safer, or left for the continent.

Patrick Hamilton, a nephew of the Earl of Arran and of the Duke of Albany, was the first to die. Influenced by Luther, he began to preach with great boldness, exposing and condemning the things that were so clearly wrong in the church. The clergy were alarmed, especially James Beaton, Archbishop of St Andrews. Because of Hamilton's social rank Beaton was afraid to take action against him openly, but he succeeded in decoying him to St Andrews on the pretext of a discussion on doctrine and on the errors of the church. When it became apparent that Hamilton would not give up his beliefs he was condemned as a heretic and burnt at the stake. On 29 February 1528, Patrick Hamilton died proclaiming, 'It is the truth of God for which I now suffer.'

The church authorities thought that by their action, the reforming movement would be suppressed. But they were wrong. 'Almost within the whole realm', writes Knox in his *History of the Reformation*, 'there were found none hearing of that fact who began not to enquire, "Wherefore was Master Patrick burned?" And when his Articles of Accusation were rehearsed, question was holden [debated], if such Articles were necessary to be believed under pain of damnation. And so within short space, many began to call in doubt that which before they held for a certain truth.'

The most outstanding of the martyrs was George Wishart. He was born around the year 1514, but little is known of him until 1538 when he had to escape to England for teaching the Greek New Testament to his students. Wishart was to remain in England for six years, studying at Cambridge. When he returned to Scotland in 1544 he preached God's word with great power in many different places and a deep impression was made on the people. But like Hamilton, his days were numbered. The chief dignitary of the church was now Cardinal David Beaton, nephew of Archbishop James Beaton. He too hated the reforming movement, and after subjecting Wishart to a mockery of a trial in St Andrews, he had him burnt at the stake on 1 March 1546.

A deep sense of outrage was felt. Knox commented, 'After the death of this Blessed Martyr of God, began the people in plain speaking to damn and detest the cruelty that was used.'

Hamilton and Wishart, along

with the many others who suffered martyrdom, did much to further the cause of reform. So did those whose lives were preserved. But no one did more than John Knox. It is to him above all that the thorough reformation of the Scottish church is due and it is to his life and work that we now turn.

The early years

Little is known about Knox's early life and there is even some uncertainty as to the date of his birth. The older view concluded that he was born in 1505. More recently his birth has been placed at 1513 or 1514. There is also uncertainty over his birthplace. A long-standing tradition assigns it to Gifford, a village not far from the East Lothian town of Haddington. Another tradition assigns it to Giffordgate in Haddington itself. Since in later life Knox described himself as a native of Haddington the latter tradition may well be the correct one.

Haddington stands on the River Tyne, some 27 kilometres east of Edinburgh and 64 kilometres by road northwest of Berwick-upon-Tweed. It was built as a Royal Burgh in the 12th century and is surrounded by some of the richest agricultural land in Scotland. Cromwell's soldiers leapt with joy when they saw it a century after Knox because: 'it contained the greatest plenty of corn they ever saw.' Like all Scottish towns of that time, Haddington would have been a very dirty place, with pigs running freely in the unpaved streets, and refuse from the houses lying about in great heaps. It had also seen

Above: Site of the house in which Knox is traditionally thought to have been born in Haddington. Beneath the oak tree beyond the gates lies a stone with the following inscription: 'Near this spot stood the house in which was born John Knox AD 1505. In commemoration an oak tree was here planted 29th March 1881 after the wish of the late Thomas Carlyle'

many changes. Haddington lay on the route of invading English armies and over the centuries suffered a great deal in the conflicts between Scotland and England. It was burned by King John of England in 1216, by King Henry III in 1241, by King Edward III in 1333 and again in 1356, and in 1548–49 the English occupied it for eighteen months in what was the longest siege in English and Scottish history. During that siege the beautiful St Mary's Church, where Knox was reader and where Wishart preached his final sermon, was extensively damaged. It remained a semi-ruin for over five hundred years until it was restored in the 1970s.

According to one of Knox's adversaries he was 'born of obscure parents'. In an interview with the Earl of Bothwell who had estates in the Haddington area, Knox himself says that his grandfathers and his father had served the Earl's predecessors, and some had died under the Bothwell standard. His father William was probably a farmer and may possibly have been killed at the battle of Flodden in 1517. We read of only one other child, Knox's brother William, who seems to have been a successful merchant. William owned a ship in which he traded with England.

The details of Knox's education are hazy. He probably attended Haddington Grammar School studying afterwards, according to a famous contemporary George Buchanan, at St Andrews University. Admittedly his name does not appear on the St Andrews University roll of graduates but that may either be because he did not finish his course or more likely because the record of his graduation disappeared. The university records were not always

Above: *Giffordgate, Haddington. The house in which Knox is traditionally thought to have been born was situated a few hundred metres along the street on the left hand side*

Above: Though extensively altered over the years, Nungate Bridge dates from at least the thirteenth century. It connects Haddington with Giffordgate. Knox would have played on it as a boy

well kept at this time.

When still a young man Knox was ordained as a priest of the Roman Catholic Church, though exactly when, or by whom, it is impossible to say. He also held the important position of a papal notary—a kind of lawyer—and as such could authenticate legal documents. In one such document, dated 27 March 1543, he describes himself as 'John Knox, minister of the Sacred Altar, of the Diocese of St Andrews, notary by Papal authority.'

It was probably in the same year, 1543, that Knox left his notarial work to become the tutor for Francis and Alexander, the sons of Hugh Douglas of Longniddry, and Alexander, son of

John Cockburn of Ormiston. Since Douglas and Cockburn had both embraced those gospel truths that the Church was seeking to suppress, Knox's decision to live with them and tutor their boys in all likelihood indicates his own acceptance of these truths.

In common with other Scottish Reformers Knox was reticent in speaking about his spiritual experience. We know that on his deathbed he asked his wife to read to him the seventeenth chapter of John's Gospel where, he said, 'I first cast my anchor'. The prayer of Christ in that chapter clearly played a key role in bringing him to faith. We know, too, that a converted Black Friar named Thomas Gwilliam had a major influence on him. According to the

historian David Calderwood, Gwilliam 'was the first man from whom Mr Knox received any taste of the truth.' But the person to whom Knox was most indebted was the martyr George Wishart. During the last five weeks of Wishart's life, Knox was his constant companion and benefited greatly by his sermons and private instructions. He was also Wishart's bodyguard. Ever since an assassination attempt on Wishart in Dundee, Knox had carried around with him a two-handed sword for the reformer's protection. Knox was with him in St Mary's Church, Haddington, on the December night in 1545 when Wishart preached his final sermon and Knox wanted to accompany him to the house where he was arrested. However, Wishart had a sense of foreboding as to what was going to happen and refused: 'Return to your bairns [children]

and God bless you! One is sufficient for a sacrifice.'

For the next fifteen months, until Easter 1547, Knox continued teaching the sons of Douglas and Cockburn. It was not an easy time for him. The persecutors of Wishart were now hunting for him. He was a marked man and had to move from place to place for his own safety, his young pupils in hiding with him. At last, becoming weary of it all, he made up his mind to leave Scotland altogether and seek refuge in Germany. Instead, however, he took a step that was to have momentous consequences both for himself and the whole reforming movement in the land. At the earnest appeal of Douglas and Cockburn he took their sons with him to the Castle of St Andrews, which by this time had become a refuge for the persecuted friends of reform.

The murder of Cardinal Beaton

St Andrews Castle had earlier been the home of Cardinal David Beaton and it was here that Beaton came to a violent end. Early one morning in May a small party of men led by William Kirkcaldy of Grange, entered the castle. The drawbridge had been down to allow materials for building work to be carried in. A little later another group entered, and then a third. At this the guard became suspicious and attempted to raise the drawbridge but he was seized and thrown into the moat. Realising that something was wrong the Cardinal barricaded himself into his room. But entry was gained by his assassins and no mercy was shown to him. He died saying, 'I am a priest, I am a priest: fye, fye, [shame] all is gone.' His body was suspended from the battlements for a while, and then placed in a coffin and lowered into the castle's notorious Bottle Dungeon.

Having murdered a man who was not only a cardinal and an archbishop, but also the chancellor of the realm, the Castilians—as those seeking refuge in the castle were called—were in peril now of their own lives. They decided to stay where they were. Others quickly joined them so that in a short time the number holding the castle rose to between 120 and 150 men. Regent Arran, the governor of Scotland at the time, besieged the castle until the end of January 1547—but he failed to take it. Not only did he have inadequate support, but his son was a hostage in the castle, and the castle was well fortified and well supplied with munitions and food. Eventually the siege was suspended. On the part of the Castilians there was an agreement to hold the castle for the Regent

Facing page: St Mary's Church and Nungate Bridge

Left: Cardinal David Beaton

William Tyndale

During Knox's early years, one of God's primary means of furthering the work of reformation in Scotland (and England) was William Tyndale's English translation of the New Testament. Unlike John Wycliffe (c.1330 – 1384), whose earlier translation of the Scriptures was based on the Latin Vulgate version, Tyndale (born c.1494) worked from the original languages. His translation of the New Testament from Greek into English was first published in 1526. A revised edition was published in 1534. It not only had a profound impact on the movement for reform in the church, but also on future English versions. A staggering ninety per cent of the King James/Authorised Version of the New Testament comes from Tyndale's 1534 edition with hardly anything altered but the spelling. Tyndale also learned Hebrew and translated parts of the Old Testament, including the Pentateuch. Tyndale was martyred in 1536.

Above: Tyndale's Bible. (The Tyndale New Testament was the first ever printed in the English language. Its first printing occurred in 1525/6, but only two complete copies of that first printing are known to have survived)

and not to hand it over to England. On the part of the Regent there was an agreement to withdraw his forces to the south of the Firth of Forth. The plan—at least on paper—was for Arran to obtain a papal pardon for those involved in the Cardinal's murder. The castle would afterwards be handed over and the Castilians would have their property restored to them.

The truce lasted from January to June 1547. During that time the occupants of the castle were permitted to come and go as they pleased. Others could join them if they wished—and they did. The castle for a time became a sanctuary for those who were seeking refuge from oppressors in Church or State. And as we have noted, Knox and his three pupils were amongst them. They entered the castle on April 10th and it was there, shortly afterwards, that Knox was called to be a preacher and to begin what was to be his life's principal work.

1. Haddington

The county town of East Lothian, Haddington is situated approximately 29 kilometres (17 miles) east of Edinburgh and 64 kilometres (39 miles) northwest of Berwick-upon-Tweed. By car, follow the A1 east from Edinburgh or north from Berwick-upon-Tweed. Haddington has no train station. For details of regular bus service, contact First Edinburgh, ☎ 0131 313 1515 or Traveline, ☎ 0131 225 3858

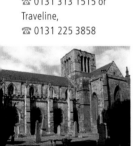

Above: *The former Knox Institute, Knox Place, Haddington converted into flats in 1985. The statue depicts Knox wearing a Geneva gown. The statue was carved by DW Stevenson in the nineteenth century*

St Mary's Church

St Mary's Church, which was consecrated circa.1400, is open daily from Easter to October 1000–1600 hrs and on Sundays 1300–1600 hrs. Guided tours are available and there is a shop and tea-room.

John Brown of Haddington

Author of 'The Self-Interpreting Bible' and numerous other works, Brown was the minister of a Scottish Secession congregation in Haddington from 1751 till his death. He combined with his pastoral duties the training of men for his denomination's ministry.

Tourist Information

For tourist information contact the Edinburgh Tourist Information Centre, ☎ 0131 473 3800 or visit their website: www.visitscotland.com

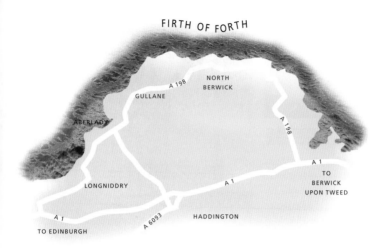

KEY TO PLACES

1 SITE OF KNOX'S BIRTHPLACE

2 ST MARY'S CHURCH

3 NUNGATE

4 KNOX INSTITUTE, KNOX PLACE

5 JOHN BROWN COURT

6 AWARD WINNING TOILETS!

7 PARKING AREA

2. St Andrews
Travel

St Andrews is situated approximately 107 kilometres (67 miles) northeast of Edinburgh (via the Forth Bridge) and 19 kilometres (12 miles) southeast of Dundee. By car from Edinburgh, travel north on the M90 to junction 8 and then take the A91 to St Andrews. Driving south from Dundee, cross the Tay Bridge and follow the signs for St Andrews and the A91.

The nearest train station is at Leuchars, which is on the main east coast Edinburgh to Aberdeen line. St Andrews is 15 minutes away by taxi or bus. For train times, ☎ National Rail, 08457 484950. For details of

regular bus services to St Andrews, ☎ 01334 474238 or City Link, 08705 505050

The Castle

A brief history

The main residence of the bishops of St Andrews, there has been a castle on this site since the 12th century.

In 1296 the castle fell into English hands and in ▶

Above: *John Brown's Court, which is situated between Newton Port and Hardgate, Haddington. This former church, dating from 1806, is built on the site of John Brown's church. On the right of the picture is a wall of the house that replaced Brown's manse*

Left: *Scene of Hamilton's martyrdom outside St Salvator's Chapel*

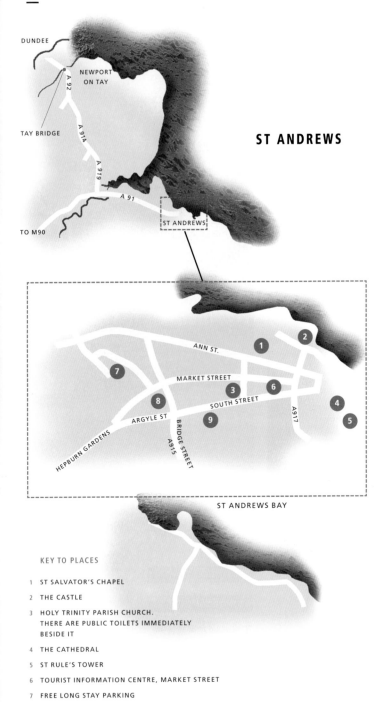

ST ANDREWS

KEY TO PLACES

1 ST SALVATOR'S CHAPEL

2 THE CASTLE

3 HOLY TRINITY PARISH CHURCH.
   THERE ARE PUBLIC TOILETS IMMEDIATELY
   BESIDE IT

4 THE CATHEDRAL

5 ST RULE'S TOWER

6 TOURIST INFORMATION CENTRE, MARKET STREET

7 FREE LONG STAY PARKING

8 PARKING

9 BLACKFRIARS CHAPEL

◁ 1303 was made ready to receive the English King. After Bannockburn in 1314 the castle was retaken and repaired by Bishop William Lamberton.

By the 1330s it was once more in English hands. In 1337 Sir Andrew Moray, Regent of Scotland, recaptured the castle after a siege lasting three weeks. The castle was then destroyed to prevent it falling into English hands.

Towards the end of the fourteenth century Bishop Walter Trail ordered that the castle be rebuilt. This was to be the basis of all further development of the castle.

In March 1546 David Beaton burnt the preacher George Wishart in front of the castle walls. He made many enemies and in May of 1546 he was murdered by a group of Fife Lairds.

After his murder the Earl of Arran ordered that the castle be sieged. Nevertheless there was an armistice which allowed the Protestant reformer John Knox the freedom to enter the castle. The armistice was broken when a French fleet arrived and started bombarding the castle. They were joined by guns firing from the towers of St Salvator's and the cathedral.

The defeated garrison including John Knox were condemned to the Galleys.

Cardinal Beaton was succeeded by Archbishop Hamilton who put right the damage caused by the siege of 1547.

St Andrews Castle is in the care of Historic Scotland and is open daily. There is wheelchair access to the castle Visitor Centre which has an interesting exhibition about the history of the castle and the cathedral. For details of opening times and admission charges, ☎ 01334 472563.

Tourist Information

The St Andrews Tourist Information Centre is in Market Street. ☎ 01334 472021

John Brown's grave Haddington

Above: *The centre stone marks John Brown's grave and is situated approx. 30 yards west of the west door of St Mary's Church. The inscription reads: 'To the memory of Mr John Brown, 36 years minister of the Gospel at Haddington and 20 years professor of Divinity under the Associate Synod. After maintaining an eminent character for piety, charity, learning and diligence he died rejoicing in hope of the glory of God, and admiring the riches of divine grace to himself as a sinner, the 19th day of June 1787, aged 65 years.' Inside St Mary's is John Brown's pulpit. There is also a memorial window to John Brown in St Mary's, with a plaque giving details of his family*

Left: *St Andrews Castle*

❷ Striking at the root

Reluctantly begun, Knox's early preaching ministry came swiftly to a close with the surrender of St Andrew's Castle. For the next nineteen months he was to experience the horrors of life as a French galley slave

As a tutor, Knox did far more than teach his pupils grammar and mathematics. He was anxious to ground them in Christian truth as well. To that end he used the question and answer form of a catechism and gave them lessons on the Gospel of John. When he had been living in Longniddry, this instruction had been given in public, and that continued to be his practice after his removal to St Andrews. He catechised the boys in the parish church and read to them his lectures on John in the castle chapel.

A large number of people gathered to hear him on these occasions and amongst them were Henry Balnaves and John Rough. Balnaves had been a prominent figure in Scottish politics and who for his support of the reforming movement had had to take refuge in St Andrews castle; John Rough was the preacher to the garrison. Both men were deeply impressed with Knox's obvious abilities and urged him to become Rough's colleague in the work of preaching. But Knox refused because he did not feel that God had called him to such work and: 'he would not run where God had not called him.'

Facing page Portrait of Henry VIII (1491-1547), c.1590 (oil on panel) by English School (16th century)

Above: St Andrews Castle

Called to preach

Rough and Balnaves were not prepared to let the matter go. They consulted with others, and unknown to Knox took the decision to issue him with a public call in the name of the whole congregation. On the day they had fixed for the purpose, Rough preached a sermon on the election of ministers. He declared that a congregation had the authority to call a man whom they recognized as having the appropriate preaching gifts, and that it was a dangerous thing for a man to refuse such a call. Rough turned to Knox, who had been listening to the sermon, and addressed him directly: 'Brother, ye shall not be offended, albeit that I speak unto you that which I have in charge, even from all those here present: In the name of God, and of his Son Jesus Christ, and in the name of these that presently call you by my mouth, I charge you, that ye refuse not this holy vocation, but, as ye tender the glory of God, the increase of Christ's kingdom, the edification of your brethren, and the comfort of me, oppressed by the multitude of labours, that ye take upon you the public office of preaching, even as ye look to avoid God's heavy displeasure, and desire that he shall multiply his graces upon you.' Turning then to the congregation, Rough continued, 'Was not this your charge to me? Do ye not approve this call?' They replied, 'It was; and we approve it.'

Knox was overwhelmed. He burst into tears, left the place of meeting, and shut himself up in his room. For days he kept himself alone and found no pleasure in anything. Some have accused him of cowardice, but the truth is very different. Few things are more striking in Knox's history than his courage. At his graveside, the Earl of Morton could say, 'Here lyeth a man who, in his life, never feared the face of man.' Knox shrinking from the office of a preacher is better to be explained in terms of a profound sensitivity to its duties and responsibilities, especially at a time when reformation was so urgently needed. He had greatly admired George Wishart and it was no light task for him to follow in Wishart's footsteps and undertake the preaching of the word of God. Nevertheless, having now received God's call through the congregation, he was not disobedient to it. From that time forward, Knox's chief work was that of a preacher.

Above: Portrait of John Knox

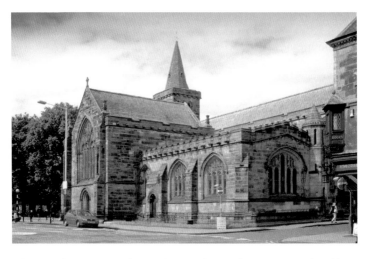

Above: Holy Trinity Parish Church, St Andrews where Knox catechised his pupils and preached his first sermon in 1547

The first sermon

John Rough was engaged in a controversy with a Roman Catholic dean named John Annand and he was assisted in this by Knox who offered to prove, in speech or in writing, that the Church of Rome had degenerated further from the purity of the apostolic church than had the Jews from the law of Moses at the time they crucified Jesus. The people realised that if Knox's charge was true, they had been completely deceived in their beliefs; they insisted that the proof be given audibly since they could not all read his writings. On the following Sunday, along with university staff and a large number of the clergy, the congregation gathered in the parish church to hear Knox preach for the first time.

According to a contemporary description, this new preacher was a man: 'rather under the middle height, with broad shoulders, swarthy face, black hair, and a beard of the same colour a span-and-a-half long. He had heavy eyebrows, beneath which the eyes were deeply sunk, while the cheekbones were prominent and the cheeks ruddy. The mouth was large, and the lips full, especially the upper one. The whole aspect of the man was not unpleasing; and in moments of emotion, it was invested with an air of dignity and majesty.'

Knox took as his text Daniel 7:24–25 and in the course of his sermon denounced the papal system as nothing less than antichristian. From Roman Catholic sources he showed how scandalously the popes lived, and from the New Testament how far from God's revealed truth they were in their doctrines, laws, titles, and claims. He ended by announcing that if anyone present disagreed with his interpretation of Scripture, he would discuss the matter with him afterwards and seek to show that the things he had taught were in accordance with the truth. The sermon created a sensation. Some said, 'Others sned [lop off] the branches of the papistry, but he striketh at the root also, to destroy the whole.' Others declared, 'Master George Wishart never spoke so plainly; and yet he was burnt. Even so will John Knox be.'

If they had had it in their power, the church authorities would have silenced Knox for ever. However, with a garrison of soldiers still occupying the castle that was not possible. The next best thing was to try and limit his influence. Orders were given that all the learned men of the abbey and the university should take it in turns to preach in the parish church on Sundays, when the largest numbers could be expected to attend. Knox was thus restricted to preaching on weekdays. Nevertheless, his preaching was very effective. In the space of a few months the inhabitants of the castle, together with many of the townspeople, formally renounced Roman Catholicism and made open profession of the Reformed faith by participating in the Lord's Supper instead of the Mass.

Shortly after this it appears that John Rough left St Andrews castle and since the re-imposition of the siege prevented his return, for a time he preached in Carlisle. Later, along with many others, he suffered martyrdom during the reign of Queen Mary (Bloody Mary) of England. With Rough's departure Knox became sole minister to the Castilians. There was certainly much to encourage him as he continued his teaching and preaching. God was evidently at work in the town and the truth was gaining ground. But amongst the soldiers occupying the castle there were instances of gross misconduct and it made Knox apprehensive as to the final outcome of the conflict. In the event his fears proved to be well grounded. At the end of June 1547 the siege of the castle was resumed and on the last day of July the occupants were forced to surrender. A key factor in governor Arran's victory was the assistance of a French fleet of twenty galleys under the command of Admiral Leone Strozzi. The castle was thus besieged both from land and sea and with no help arriving from England, the forces ranged against it were too much for its defences.

England, Scotland and France— political intrigue

Back in 1531, King Henry VIII of England broke with the Pope and declared himself head of the English Church. In this he stood largely alone since most other countries of Europe remained loyal to the Pope. Afraid that these countries would some day unite against him in war, Henry was very anxious to have Scotland on his side and did all that he could to make an ally of the Scottish king, James V.

He tried to get James to marry his daughter, the Princess Mary,

Above: John Knox dispensing the Lord's Supper in St Andrews, 1547

who was afterwards Queen Mary of England, but James refused. He had his suspicions that Henry's real aim was to make himself king of both England and Scotland and for that reason preferred friendship with France. James also had greater religious sympathies with France since France was also determined to remain loyal to the Pope. The relations between Scotland and France were strengthened in 1537 when James married Madeleine, a daughter of the French king, Francis I; they were further strengthened in 1538 when, after Madeleine's death, James married another French noblewoman, Mary of Lorraine (Mary of Guise).

In 1542 the English inflicted a humiliating defeat on the Scots' army at Solway Moss. Ill and broken-hearted, James took to his bed in Falkland Palace and died shortly after. His one week old daughter, Mary, became queen (Mary Queen of Scots), with the Earl of Arran acting as Regent. Arran had sympathies at that time with the reforming or Protestant movement and for that reason favoured relations with Protestant England rather than with Roman Catholic France. When Henry VIII proposed that a marriage be arranged between the infant Mary and his five-year-old son Edward VI, Arran was in agreement. With the help of certain Scottish nobles and gentlemen, Arran succeeded in persuading the Scottish Parliament to accept this proposal. And so, by the treaty of Greenwich, signed on 1 July 1543, it was determined that Mary

Above:James V of Scotland (1512-42),

Opposite: Knox on board the galley, looking over to St Andrews

would marry Edward when she was eleven years of age and that in the meantime there was to be peace between the two countries.

Many Scottish people were unhappy about this, suspecting Henry of wishing to make himself Scotland's ruler. Two persons in particular were alarmed: Mary of Lorraine, the infant queen's mother, and Cardinal David Beaton. Those two were determined that Scotland should remain both Catholic and the ally of France. Beaton was one of the most powerful and wealthy men in the country, and most of the nobles and people were on his side. Through his influence the whole situation changed. The

Scottish Parliament broke off the marriage treaty with England, Arran distanced himself from the reforming movement, and severe laws against those involved in that movement were re-enacted. Meanwhile, Henry VIII took his revenge. Furious at the defeat of his plans, he invaded Scotland in 1544 and again in 1545, leaving destruction and misery in his wake.

Scotland of the 1540s was thus a divided and troubled country. On the one hand there were many who favoured alliance with France and the maintenance of the old Roman Catholic religion. On the other hand there was a growing number whose preference was for an alliance with England. Such an alliance would bring an end to the misery of English invasions. It would secure far greater freedom, too, for the work of reformation.

Against this background we can appreciate the events that took place in St Andrews. During the first part of the siege, the Castilians looked to England for help and in fact received it. In November 1546 an English fleet brought them provisions. Negotiators were then sent back with the fleet with authority to enter into an alliance with Henry VIII. But nothing came of their efforts. During the second part of the siege in July 1547, the Castilians again looked for English help but none came. What arrived instead was a French fleet under Admiral Strozzi.

Galley slave
The Castilians succeeded in badly damaging one of the ships and so

effective was the castle's cannon that the French fleet sailed for safety to Dundee. But when Strozzi resumed his attack with cannon placed in St Andrews itself, a breach was soon blown in the castle's curtain wall. Knox had warned the Castilians that 'their walls were no better than eggshells' and so they proved. A plague also broke out in the castle itself, leaving the occupants with no choice but to negotiate a surrender.

The terms were that in return for giving up the castle they would all be allowed to live—but not in Scotland. They would be taken to France where they could remain if they wished, or leave at French expense for any country other than Scotland. But the promises were not kept. No one was executed, but there was to be no freedom in France. At the request of both the Pope and governor Arran, the prisoners were

condemned to perpetual captivity, the nobles in various castles, the others in the galleys. Knox was sent to the galleys and there he remained for the next nineteen months, a slave in chains.

The name of the galley in which Knox worked was the Nostre Dame [Our Lady]. It was part of a fleet that was stationed at Rouen during the summer months and at Nantes on the Loire during the winter. Its job was to protect the French coast from English raids. Twice during Knox's captivity the Nostre Dame also carried French troops to Scotland. One of Knox's biographers has given us a vivid description of galley life: 'The average galley was one hundred and fifty feet long with a beam of fifty feet. At the stern was a small cabin for the captain and another for the stores. Down the length of the centre of the ship ran a raised walk between the slaves' benches for the overseer who could urge on by word and blows those lagging in the rowing. Usually propelled by twenty-five oars to a side, the galley would carry about three hundred slaves who worked six to an oar, each chained to his bench. At night on shipboard they slept either on the benches or on the floor, while during the day, since the galleys were only partially decked, they either roasted in the sun or shivered in the rain or cold winds. There was little food either and nothing by way of sanitation or privacy. The stench on board was appalling and galley-fever rife. It was a terrible place to be.'

Every effort was made to persuade the Scottish prisoners

to embrace Roman Catholicism. But it was wholly in vain. In spite of their sufferings they all remained faithful to the truth and refused to give any support to error. Knox relates a humorous incident in which he himself was probably the person concerned: 'Soon after their arrival at Nantes, a glorious painted Lady [an image of the Virgin Mary] was brought in to be kissed, and, amongst others, was presented to one of the Scottishmen then chained. He gently said, "Trouble me not. Such an idol is accursed; therefore I will not touch it." The Captain and the Lieutenant, with two officers, having the chief charge of all such matters, said, "Thou shalt handle it"—and they violently thrust it to his face, and put it betwixt his hands. He… took the idol, and advisedly looking about him, cast it into the river, and said, "Let our Lady now save herself. She is light enough; let her learn to swim!" After that was no Scotsman urged with that idolatry!'

Knox's experiences in the galley did lasting damage to his health. Constant pain and weakness were to be his for the rest of his life. On the galley he was so ill at one point that many despaired of his life. But Knox himself was confident that he would survive. It was his conviction from the beginning of his captivity that one day he and the other Scots prisoners would be freed: 'God will deliver us from this bondage, to His glory, even in this life.' Not that he was free of moments of darkness. In a work entitled *A Declaration of the True Nature and Object of Prayer,* he speaks of a time when 'in anguish of mind and vehement tribulation and affliction I called to the Lord, when not only the ungodly but

Above: St Andrews Castle from St Rules Tower

Left: A Victorian depiction of Knox casting overboard an image of Mary "Let our Lady now save herself. She is light enough; let her learn to swim!"
(Note that Knox has been incorrectly shown as clean-shaven)

even my faithful brethren, yea, and my own self, judged my cause to be irremediable.' Nevertheless the conviction that he would eventually be free remained. The galley was lying off St Andrews at the time with the town just visible. His fellow prisoner, James Balfour, raised him up and asked him if he knew the place. 'Yes', he answered; 'I know it well. I see the steeple of that place where God first in public opened my mouth to His glory, and I am fully persuaded, how weak soever I now appear, I shall not depart this life till my tongue shall glorify His Holy Name in the same place.' And so it proved. After nineteen months as a prisoner he was released along with the others. And the day came when the parish church of St Andrews echoed once again to the sound of his preaching.

TRAVEL DETAILS

St Andrews

For street map and for information about travel, the tourist centre, and St Andrews Castle and Visitor Centre see details at the close of chapter 1.

The Parish Church

Holy Trinity Parish Church, dating from the early 15th century, is only open during times of public worship.

St Rule's Tower

The 12th century St Rule's Tower, originally part of an Augustinian Priory, is in the cathedral grounds. It is in the care of Historic Scotland and is open daily. There are superb views from the top over the whole town. Access to the cathedral grounds is free but there is an admission charge for the Tower. ☎ 01334 472563 for further details.

❸ 'That great rest'

Released at last from his captivity, Knox began again to preach. But not in his native Scotland. For five years he ministered in England where he saw a town transformed by his preaching, met his future wife, and became a chaplain to young King Edward VI

Early in 1549 Knox gained his freedom. There is no certainty as to how it came about, though one possibility is that he was released on the orders of the French King after representations were made to him by some of Knox's friends that Knox had had no hand in Cardinal Beaton's murder. But however it happened, he and the other Castilians found themselves free men at last. The question that now faced Knox was where to go. To have followed his heart and returned at this point to Scotland would undoubtedly have meant arrest, trial, and death. And so, since England at this point in time was a far safer place for the friends of the reforming movement, the decision was taken to sail for England. He remained there for five years.

There had been significant changes in England since the time of Cardinal Beaton's death. Henry VIII died on 28 January 1547 and was succeeded by his young son, Edward VI. This ushered in a time of considerable religious freedom. The Lord Protector, the Duke of Somerset, was in sympathy with those who were eager for

Above: Portrait of Thomas Cranmer (1489-1556) from 'Lodge's British Portraits', 1823 (litho) by Gerlach Flicke (fl.1547-58) (after)

Facing page The Cathedral Church of St Nicholas in Newcastle where Knox preached, 1551–1553. Regrettably, there is nothing in the church that commemorates this ministry

reformation, and the Archbishop of Canterbury, Thomas Cranmer, was a firm friend of the truth.

So too was the new king. Knox had the highest regard for Edward and described him as 'that most godly and virtuous king'; he spoke of the brief years of his reign as 'that great rest'. Religious refugees from the continent poured into the country and for Knox himself there was soon found a sphere of activity. His name occurs as sixty-fourth in a list of eighty men who obtained licence to preach in England during Edward's reign, and around April 1549 Knox was appointed to the border town of Berwick-upon-Tweed.

Berwick-upon-Tweed

The Berwick of those days was a turbulent and unruly place. With the ongoing conflict between England and Scotland, its garrison was larger than usual and quarrels among the soldiers were common. A contemporary report declares, 'There is better order among the Tartars than in this town; the whole picture of the place is one of social disorder.' It was no easy place for a preacher to be assigned to.

In the days before the Reformation, Berwick had four churches: the Church of St Lawrence, the Church of the Blessed Mary, the Church of

Above: Berwick Parish Church. The Parish Church in which Knox preached was situated in the foreground of the picture where the gravestones are. It lay parallel to the present church

Facing page: Norham Castle, near Berwick-upon-Tweed

St Nicholas, and the Church of the Holy Trinity. The last named was Berwick's parish church and it was to this church that Knox was appointed. It was very small. When in 1641 a petition was presented to King Charles I for a new church he was informed that the people of Berwick 'were necessitated to make use of a very little church, meanly built, with not room enough for half the inhabitants'. The present parish church, completed in 1652, replaced it.

The vicar when Knox was appointed was Sir Robert Selby. Like so many of the clergy of that time he played no direct part in the work of his parish, leaving it instead to a curate. This man, to whom Selby paid seven pounds a year, is described as 'a very simple man, devoid of all learning'. Selby himself was said to be 'more ignorant than the curate', and it was doubted whether he could say the Lord's Prayer either in Latin or English. The Dean of Durham declared him unfit 'to take any care of Christian people'.

In Knox, however, the citizens of Berwick had a man of a very different stamp. In 1552, a year after his Berwick ministry closed, Knox wrote a letter to his old congregation. It sheds a revealing light on the truths that they heard from his lips. He had taught them about God's choice of sinners through 'his own infinite goodness and mere mercy' alone; about Jesus, the only 'name under the heaven wherein salvation stands'; and about justification 'by faith only'. He had insisted that prayers be made to no other than 'God above', that there is no 'mediator betwixt God and man, but only our Lord Jesus', that there are no other sacraments than 'Baptism and the Lord's Table', and that the 'remission of sins, resurrection of the flesh and life everlasting' comes to people only through 'Christ's blood, which, sprinkled in our hearts by faith, doth purge us from all sin.' These were the fundamental truths that were preached to the Berwick people, and to great effect. A change took place in the town so marked that Knox at a later date could say to Mary, Queen of Scots: 'I shame not, Madame, further to affirm that God so blessed my weak labours that in Berwick (where commonly before there used to be slaughter by reason of quarrels arising among the soldiers) there was as great quietness all the time that I remained there as there is this day in Edinburgh.'

Marjory Bowes

The time Knox spent in Berwick was good not only for the people but for the preacher himself. It gave him experience for the first time of a settled pastoral ministry. He had time to read and study, something that he had known little of since the days at Longniddry. With the galleys behind him there may well have been some improvement in his health, although he did have difficulty sleeping at night because of pain. It was also in Berwick that Knox met and fell in love with Marjory Bowes. She was a daughter of Richard Bowes, Captain of nearby Norham Castle, and his wife Elizabeth.

Marjory's mother, who attended Knox's preaching in the

Above: High Street, Rochester

Left: After Canterbury Cathedral, Rochester's Norman Cathedral is the oldest in the country

Above: South East view of Norham Castle

parish church and identified with the reforming cause, thoroughly approved of the match. However, her father did not. He objected probably on account of Knox's Protestant beliefs. The difficulties were eventually overcome and to the couple's great happiness the marriage was able to take place—though when and in what circumstances is now no longer known.

A correspondence began between Knox and Marjory's mother, Elizabeth, and a large number of their letters have been preserved. She was subject to spiritual depression and often doubted whether a work of grace had taken place in her life. It was on such matters that she wrote to her future son-in-law, who in his replies sought gently to counsel and encourage her. Thus in one letter, written from Carlisle in 1553, he encouraged her: 'The manifold and general assaults of the devil raging against you, and troubling your rest, while you thirst and most earnestly desire to remain in Christ, doth certify unto me your very election, which the devil envies in all the chosen of God.' In another, sent from Newcastle in the same year, he writes, 'In my conscience I judge, and by the Holy Spirit of my God am fully certified, that you are a member of Christ's body, sore troubled and vexed presently, that the lusts and vain pleasures of the flesh mortified, you may shortly rest, and rise hereafter in honour and glory…Wherefore persevere. Albeit the battle be strong, yet the glory of your deliverance may be ascribed, and wholly given to God.' In words like these Knox tried to comfort this troubled believer. They reveal a tender and caring heart, and great skill in dealing with a Christian's inner conflicts. The letters also gave Knox a forum in which to pour out his own troubles and to solicit Mrs Bowes' prayers.

In his lifetime, Knox's enemies took advantage of this frequent correspondence to suggest that there was something improper in his relationship with Mrs Bowes. The innuendos were firmly rebutted, and after Elizabeth's death Knox declared that the 'cause of their great familiarity and long acquaintance' was 'neither flesh nor blood, but a troubled conscience upon her part, which never suffered her to rest but when she was in the company of the faithful, of whom (from the first hearing of the word at my mouth) she judged me to be one.'

Newcastle

Knox remained in Berwick for a further year and then in the early summer of 1551 he moved to the Church of St Nicholas in Newcastle.

This extended the sphere of his influence. His congregation was larger than the one he had in Berwick, there was scope for preaching in other places in the north, and he was immensely popular—particularly with his fellow Scots. When the following year the Duke of Northumberland recommended that Knox be offered the bishopric of Rochester in Kent, it was partly from a wish to reduce the number of Scots who were coming to Newcastle to sit under Knox's preaching! If he was appointed to Rochester, a great distance away in the southeast of the country: 'The family of the Scots now inhabiting in Newcastle, chiefly for his fellowship, would not continue there, wherein many resort to them out of Scotland, which is not requisite [necessary].'

In a letter to his Newcastle friends, written from the continent in 1558, Knox gives us an insight into the character of this popular Newcastle ministry: 'God is witness, and I refuse not your own judgements, how simply and uprightly I conversed and walked among you, that neither for fear did I spare to speak the simple truth unto you; neither for hope of worldly promotion, dignity, or honour, did I wittingly adulterate any part of God's Scriptures, whether it were in exposition, in preaching, contention, or writing; but that simply and plainly, as it pleased the merciful goodness of my God to give me utterance, understanding, and spirit, I did distribute the bread of life, as of Christ Jesus I had received it. I sought neither pre-eminence, glory nor riches. My honour was that Christ Jesus should reign, my glory that the light of his truth should shine in you, and my greatest riches that in the same ye should be constant.'

Chaplain to the King

In December 1551, just months after Knox's arrival in Newcastle, six men were appointed as chaplains to King Edward VI. They were selected because they were 'accounted the most zealous and ready preachers of the time.'

Left: Mary Tudor, Queen of England 1553–1558

Two of them in turn would be present with the king; the others would spend their time touring the country as itinerant preachers. Each would receive a salary of £40 per annum, a sizeable sum in those days. There is evidence that points to one of these chaplains being Knox himself. The appointment would have raised his profile considerably and extended still further his influence as a preacher.

During the final few months of 1552, Knox spent some unhappy months in London. The king was ill, and Knox had growing fears for the future. What he saw in the lives of those who occupied positions of influence sickened and alarmed him, for not only were there the inevitable power struggles, it was apparent that if the king died many would come out strongly on the side of Catholicism. The 'great rest' would be over. He returned to Newcastle at the end of December 1552 and on Christmas Day gave vent to his fears in a powerful sermon. He lamented the obstinacy of the enemies of the gospel, accusing them of being secret traitors to the crown and commonwealth who were thirsting for the king's death. It was all too apparent, he said, that they did not care who reigned in Edward's place, provided only the Catholic faith was restored. The reaction to this sermon on the part of Knox's opponents was so violent that but for his high standing with the king

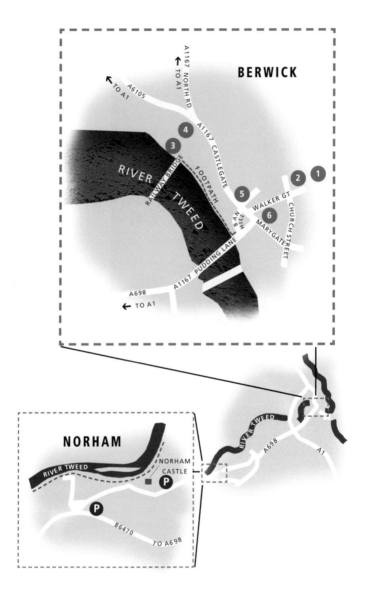

BERWICK-UPON-TWEED

1 BERWICK PARISH CHURCH

2 WALLACE GREEN CHURCH OF SCOTLAND

3 BERWICK CASTLE

4 BERWICK TRAIN STATION AND BUS STATION

5 TOWN CENTRE PARKING WITH PUBLIC TOILETS

6 TOURIST INFORMATION CENTRE, MARYGATE

Left: King Edward VI (1537-53)

STEVE DEVANE

he would have been in serious trouble.

When the offer of the bishopric of Rochester had been made to Knox, he had refused it. In February 1553 another position was offered to him: the rectorship of All-Hallows in Bread Street, London. But he declined this as well. The reformation of the Church of England had not gone far enough for him to accept a permanent charge in good conscience. In Berwick and Newcastle he seems to have been given considerable freedom to preach and to administer the Lord's Supper as he thought right. Instead of using bread that was 'unleavened and round', as the 1549 Prayer Book

instructed, Knox used common bread. Again, instead of kneeling to receive the bread and wine, the people sat. If he were to accept a bishopric or a rectorship, however, it would mean a level of conformity to the Church's beliefs and practices that was impossible for him.

Death of the King

On 6 July 1553, King Edward VI died at the age of sixteen. 'We had' said Knox, 'a king of so godly disposition towards virtue and the truth of God, that none from the beginning passed him, and to my knowledge, none of his years did ever match him.' His sister Mary was proclaimed queen on 19 July.

NEWCASTLE UPON TYNE

KEY TO PLACES

1 ST NICHOLAS CATHEDRAL

2 BLACKGATE

3 CASTLE KEEP

4 BESSIE SURTEES HOUSE

5 PUBLIC TOILETS, GROAT STREET

6 RAIL STATION, NEVILLE STREET. THERE ARE PUBLIC TOILETS AND A
TOURIST INFORMATION CENTRE AT THE STATION

7 PARKING, DEAN STREET. THERE ARE A SMALL NUMBER OF PARKING
PLACES AT THE CASTLE KEEP. PARKING IS ALSO AVAILABLE ON THE
QUAYSIDE AND IN A NUMBER OF OTHER PARTS OF THE CITY CENTRE.

Left: Church of Scotland, Wallace Green, formerly Wallace Green United Presbyterian Church. The church is only open at times of public worship

Her accession to the throne was greeted with great joy by the people of London, but amongst the friends of reform there was deep unease. Her proclamation the following month of toleration both for Protestants and Catholics gave some months of respite. But it was the calm before the storm. Mary's sympathies were entirely Roman Catholic. So were those of three-quarters of her subjects, and so were those of many in her Council. It was only to be expected, then, that toleration for Protestants would be a very temporary thing. In November Parliament repealed the laws that had been made in favour of church reform, and restored Roman Catholicism to its former position as the religion of the realm. A

month's grace was given to Protestants. Until 20 December they were to be free to engage in reformed worship. But after that they would cease to have the protection of the law, and could be arrested, tried, and punished as heretics. The 'great rest' was well and truly over. Most of the Protestant bishops and ministers were committed to prison; others fled the country. And in the following four years many of England's finest Christians would die at the stake.

But what of Knox? We know that through the summer months he was carrying on an itinerant ministry in Buckinghamshire and Kent. We know, too, that by the autumn he was back in London, where he remained for some

Above: Designed by John Young of Blackfriars, with foundation stone laid in 1650 and opened in 1652, Berwick Parish Church replaced the medieval Church which had stood a few yards to the south since 1190 and which was demolished shortly after the new church was opened.
The building is comprised largely of the stones and timbers of Edward I's once Great 13th Century Castle of Berwick-upon-Tweed

weeks. The capital becoming too dangerous for him, he then returned north to Newcastle, but he had powerful enemies there who were on the lookout for him, eager for revenge. Finally he took the painful decision to move to a place of safety on the coast from which, if necessary, he could leave the country by ship. He went, he says, because: 'his brethren had, partly by tears and partly by admonition, compelled him to obey, somewhat contrary to his own mind, for never could he die in a more honest quarrel than by suffering as a witness for that truth of which God had made him a messenger.' Later, when it became apparent that to remain in England would mean death, he followed his friends' counsel and set sail for France, landing at Dieppe on the 20 January 1554.

John Knox's feelings at the close of his five years ministry in England are well expressed in a letter written just before he boarded his ship: 'My daily prayer is for the sore afflicted in those quarters. Some time I have thought that it had been impossible so to have removed my affection from Scotland that any realm or nation could have been equally dear unto me; but I take God to witness that the troubles present and appearing to be in the realm of England are doubly dolorous [painful] unto my heart than ever were the troubles of Scotland.'

TRAVEL DETAILS

Tweed Travel

Berwick-upon-Tweed is approximately 58 miles (93 kilometres) southeast of Edinburgh and 58 miles (94 kilometres) north of Newcastle. It lies immediately south of the Scottish border and is easily accessible both by road and rail. By road, follow the A1 north from Newcastle or east from Edinburgh. For details of train services, ☎ National Rail, 08457 484950 For details of bus services, ☎ 01289 307283

Berwick Parish Church

Completed in 1652, the Parish Church is a rare example of a church built during Cromwell's Protectorate. It is open Monday to Saturday, 0830–1700 hrs. Sunday, 0730–1900 hrs.

Above: *Revd Dr John Cairns, 1818-1892*

Above: *Monument beside the Parish Church in Berwick marking the grave of the Revd Dr Robert Balmer, 1787-1844*

Dr Balmer

Dr Balmer was the minister of a Scottish Secession congregation in Berwick-upon-Tweed and also his denomination's professor of Systematic Theology. The inscription in part describes him as: 'a man of high endowments, attainments and worth, a sincere and devout Christian, an accurate and elegant scholar, a learned and sound divine, an instructive and impressive preacher, a faithful and affectionate pastor…'

Dr John Cairns

Dr Cairns was the minister of Wallace Green United Presbyterian Church, Berwick-upon-Tweed until 1876. In 1867 he was appointed Professor of Apologetics at his denomination's Theological Hall in Edinburgh and was Principal from1879 till his death. As a student he was greatly influenced by the Revd. John Brown of Edinburgh, grandson of John Brown of Haddington, and later wrote his biography.

Tourist Information

The Tourist Information Centre is on Marygate. ☎ 01289 330733

Norham Castle

12th century Norham Castle is in the care of English Heritage. It is open 1 April–30 September, 10am–6pm. It is located at Norham village, 6½ miles (10½ kilometres) SW of Berwick-upon-Tweed on the B6470. ☎ 01289 382329 for further details.

For details of the bus service from Berwick to Norham Castle and village, ☎ 01289 307283

Newcastle

Public toilets, Groat Street Train Station, Neville Street. There are public

Right: St Nicholas' Cathedral

Below: Memorial to Dr Cairns in the vestibule of the Wallace Green Church

toilets and a Tourist Information Centre at the station.
Parking, Dean Street. There are a small number of parking places at the Castle Keep. Parking is also available on the Quayside and in a number of other parts of the city centre.

Travel

By car, Newcastle is reached from the north and the south by the A1. The city centre may be reached from the south by taking the A167 exit road for Gateshead or from the north by taking the A696 exit road.
For details of train services to Newcastle, ☎ National Rail 08457 484950

For details of bus services to and in Newcastle, ☎ Traveline 0870 608 2 608

St Nicholas' Cathedral

The Cathedral is situated on the corner of Mosley Street and St Nicholas Street in the city centre and is open Monday to Friday, 0700–1800 hrs. Saturday, 0800–1600 hrs. Bank holidays, 0800–1200 hrs. Sundays, 0700–1200 hrs. 1600–1900 hrs.

THE REV. PRINCIPAL
JOHN CAIRNS, D.D.L.L.D.
MINISTER OF THIS CONGREGATION
1845 TO 1876.
BORN 23ᵈ AUGUST 1818,
DIED 12ᵗʰ MARCH 1892.

Far Left: *The Blackgate, St Nicholas Street*

Left: *Bessie Surtees House is on the Quayside beneath the Castle Keep.*

Below: *Situated on St Nicholas Street, the Castle Keep*

The Blackgate

The Blackgate is on St Nicholas Street near St Nicholas Cathedral. It was the principal gateway to the castle and was built between 1247 and 1250. It can be viewed at any time.

The Castle Keep

The Castle Keep was the principal tower of the Castle. It was built by King Henry II between 1168 and 1178. It is situated on St Nicholas Street and is open daily, 0930–1730 hrs. (April–September); 0930–1630 hrs. (October–March)

Bessie Surtees House

Bessie Surtees House is on the Quayside beneath the Castle Keep. It dates from just a few years after Knox and is a fine example of the kind of house lived in by wealthy Newcastle merchants of the time. It is in the care of English Heritage and is open Monday–Friday 1000–1600 hrs. For further details, ☎ 0191 269 1200

Tourist Information

For Newcastle Tourist Information Centre, ☎ 0191 277 8000

The Castle Keep

④ Travels, trials, and triumphs

The five years that followed Knox's departure from England were spent in various parts of continental Europe. But there was also a trip to Scotland—ever memorable to Knox for the hunger that he found there for the word of God

Knox would not have been the only Scotsman in Dieppe at that time. Because of the trading links between Scotland and France many Scots merchants had settled both in Dieppe and in other French ports. Knox may very well have known some of these merchants and found amongst them men with similar convictions to himself.

A visit to Switzerland

Knox spent only a few weeks in Dieppe and then left for Switzerland. There, as we learn from one of his letters, he visited all the congregations and held discussions with pastors and other scholars on various matters that were much on his mind at the time. Amongst those whom he consulted were John Calvin in Geneva, Pierre Viret in Lausanne, and Heinrich Bullinger in Zurich.

Knox put a series of questions to these men on issues that were of urgent relevance to the Scottish and English churches. In view of the forthcoming marriage, which took place in 1554, between Mary Tudor of England and Philip of Spain, he asked whether a woman who bore rule over a country could transfer her rights of government to her husband.

Above: Pierre Viret, 1511–71. Viret spent thirty years in Christian work in Lausanne and Geneva

Facing page: This water fountain has, over the years, grown to be the symbol of Geneva, pumping 132 gallons (500 litres) of water per second to a height of 450 feet (140 metres) at a speed of 125 miles per hour (200 km per hour)

Above: Heinrich Bullinger, 1504–75. Bullinger was chief pastor in Zurich from December 1531 onwards

Facing page: St Peter's Cathedral, Geneva 1735

Other questions had to do with the lawfulness of disobeying magistrates who were intent on enforcing conformity to Roman Catholicism and, in the case of a ruler with the same intention, whether it was lawful to support a nobility who were resisting him. The answers that Knox received to these questions were cautious, especially in regard to the matter of resistance. The continental reformers were agreed that it was better to die than to be guilty of idolatry, but they clearly had reservations about rebellion. For Bullinger, participation in such a conflict was ultimately a matter of conscience; for Calvin, the only recourse was to prayer, since violence blinded those involved in it.

Knox returned to Dieppe in May, and remained there for some months. On the last day of May he sent a 'comfortable [comforting] epistle' to the suffering believers in England, 'exhorting them to bear his cross with patience, looking every hour for his coming again, to the great comfort and consolation of his chosen.' As in an earlier 'comfortable epistle', Knox's theme was the assurance that God's deliverance of his sorely tried people was a certainty: 'And therefore, beloved brethren in our Lord Jesus Christ, seeing that neither can our imperfections nor frail weakness hinder Christ Jesus to return to us by the presence of his word; neither that the tyranny of these blood-thirsty wolves may so devour Christ's small flock, but that a great number shall be preserved to the praise of God's glory; neither that these most cruel tyrants can long escape God's vengeance, let us in comfort lift up our heads, and constantly look for the Lord's deliverance with heart and voice.'

News from England was becoming increasingly dark. The persecution of God's faithful people was gathering momentum, with more and more being forced to flee the country. It drew from Knox a strongly worded publication, his *Admonition to England*, dated 20 July 1554. As in previous letters, his concern was to encourage the believers to persevere in the face of suffering, and to reassure them of final

John Calvin

John Calvin was the most influential of the Reformation theologians. His principal work, *Institutes of the Christian Religion*, is still in print today. In this the key doctrines of the Christian faith receive comprehensive treatment. He wrote commentaries on all the books of the New Testament with the exception of Revelation, and on many Old Testament books. Besides being a prolific writer, Calvin was a powerful preacher whose ministry was largely spent in Geneva. He was deeply involved in preparing men for the Christian ministry, and students came to him in large numbers from all over the continent.

Above: John Calvin, 1509–64

victory. But the pamphlet embraces other matters. With so many deprived of the opportunity of hearing God's word he confessed that when he was with them he should have moved around the country far more than he did. There are also strong denunciations of key figures in church and state: Tunstall, Bishop of Durham; Gardiner, Bishop of Winchester; Bonner, Bishop of London; and Queen Mary herself. He referred to: 'Stephen Gardiner and his black brood' and declared that, 'the devil rageth in his obedient servants, wily Winchester, dreaming Durham, and bloody Bonner, with the rest of their bloody, butcherly brood'. He dared to denounce the Queen: 'Jezebel never erected half so many gallows in all Israel as mischievous Mary hath done

within London alone'; he condemned her as 'a breaker of promises' and 'a wicked woman'.

Not surprisingly, Knox has been censured for such strong language, and some of the criticism may be just, but it has to be borne in mind that controversy in Knox's day was commonly conducted in language like this. Account needs to be taken too of the circumstances that gave rise to the *Admonition*, and the pain of his own heart at the persecution and death of many of his friends. One biographer, William Taylor, urges us to remember that Mary, on her accession, had publicly declared that she 'meant graciously not to compel or strain other men's consciences otherwise than God should, as she trusted, put in their hearts a persuasion of the truth, through the opening of his word unto them', and that, by her subsequent conduct, she had utterly falsified that word. At the very time of Knox's writing, the English Protestant leaders Cranmer, Ridley, and Latimer were prisoners in the Tower of London on charges of treason and heresy—all were subsequently burnt. Reports were continually coming to Knox's ears of Mary's cruelty toward English Protestants, many of them his personal friends. The strength of his language, therefore, though not perhaps entirely excusable, is at least understandable.

Call to Frankfurt

Knox moved from Dieppe in August, hoping to settle and study for a while in Geneva. It had long been his ambition to learn Hebrew, and here at last was an opportunity. But the Hebrew would have to wait until a later date. In September he received a call to be one of the pastors of a congregation of English exiles in the German city of Frankfurt-on-the-Maine (now Frankfurt on Main), and though reluctant at first to accept it, he finally did so on the advice of John Calvin.

Frankfurt was one of a number of places in Europe to which the refugees from persecution had fled. There they had the use of a place of worship that was also being used by a French congregation. A certain condition had to be observed, however. In their services of worship it was required of the English congregation that they conform as closely as possible to the liturgy used by the French—a requirement that was understood to be sufficiently fulfilled if the English Prayer Book was used, with the litany and the responses left out, and with a few other modifications. It was a condition that suited Knox very well, because the parts omitted were the very ones with which he had been unhappy in England. But trouble was brewing. Other English exiles in Zurich and in Strasbourg were displeased with the changes, and by letters and deputations they stirred up dissension in the congregation. Peace was only restored after intervention by Calvin. He wrote saying how grieved he was at these 'unseemly contentions', and condemned the obstinacy of those who refused to make any changes to the old customs. He declared that in the

Left: St Peter's Cathedral, Geneva. The construction began in 1160 and lasted 150 years. The massive neoclassical facade was added in 1750

English liturgy he had found many 'tolerable fooleries', things that might be borne with when reformation was beginning, but which ought to be removed as soon as possible. Now, he thought, was an excellent time to remove them.

Regrettably, the peace was short-lived. In March 1555, Dr Richard Cox arrived in Frankfurt with others like him, and at the first service of worship they attended, they completely disregarded the agreed order of things and broke out into loud responses. On being reproved by the elders of the congregation, they replied that 'they would do as they had done in England, and they would have the face of an English church.' Worse was to come. On the following Sunday one of their number, without the knowledge or consent of the congregation, entered the pulpit and proceeded to read the Litany, while the rest answered aloud. This was too much for Knox who in the afternoon, in the course of a sermon on Genesis, rebuked the newcomers for disturbing a hard-won peace, and insisted that nothing should be introduced into worship which lacked biblical warrant. There were, he said, things in the English Prayer Book that were superstitious, impure, and imperfect, and he would oppose at every legitimate opportunity those who sought to impose them on a Christian congregation.

When the congregation met

later to discuss the matter, Cox and his associates insisted on the right to vote. The congregation disagreed, but on the intercession of Knox, who on this occasion was 'more remarkable for magnanimity than prudence', permission to vote was granted. It was immediately used against him. At the instigation of Cox, Knox was discharged from preaching and forbidden to interfere in congregational affairs. His supporters were understandably outraged, and the case was taken to the senate of Frankfurt. But in spite of the senate's intervention and evident sympathy with Knox, the situation continued to deteriorate until it was necessary to suggest to Knox that he privately withdraw from the city. On 25 March 1555, he preached a consolatory sermon to about fifty of the members, and left the next day. Some of the members accompanied him for the first three or four miles of his journey and then: 'with great heaviness of heart and plenty of tears, committed him to the Lord'.

Return to Scotland

From Frankfurt, Knox made his way to Geneva, where he was later joined by many of those who had supported him in the controversy with Cox. He was invited to resume his ministry amongst them and through Calvin's influence, the church called the Temple de Nostre Dame la Nove was made available for the English congregation.

Knox remained in Geneva for several months, but was absent on the 1 November 1555, when the English church was formally constituted. Christopher Goodman and Arthur Gilby were 'appointed to preach the word, in the absence of John Knox'. For the remainder of this chapter it is the 'absence of John Knox' that will

MIKE CLARK

MIKE CLARK

Above: *Glaciers on the Eiger*

Facing page: *Geneva; lakeside Chateau*

occupy our attention.

In response by and large to the pleas of his friend Mrs Bowes, Knox was encouraged in the autumn of 1555 to leave Geneva and return to the north of England. He admits that to begin with, the idea was 'most contrary' to his judgement, but in the overruling providence of God the months away from Geneva proved immensely helpful both to himself and to the movement for reform in Scotland.

As soon as he landed, Knox made his way to Berwick, where he was reunited with Mrs Bowes and her daughter Marjory, the young woman with whom he had fallen in love during his Berwick days. It is possible that the two of them were already married. One of Knox's biographers has argued that they married secretly as far back as 1551, before Knox moved to Newcastle, and that the marriage remained secret because of the opposition of Marjory's father. Others suggest that the marriage took place in 1553, prior to Knox's departure from England, and some that it took place between September 1555 and the summer of 1556, when Knox was in Berwick and Scotland. All that we know for certain is that they were husband and wife by 13 September 1556, for on that day, having returned from Scotland, an official register records, 'John Knox; Marjory his wife, Elizabeth her mother…were received and admitted members of the English Church and congregation' in Geneva.

The bulk of Knox's time during

his absence from Geneva was spent in Scotland. Six years had elapsed since his forced departure in the galley, and during those years the work of reformation had been making progress. Several factors contributed to this. One was undoubtedly the evangelical literature that in spite of the acts of 1525 and 1527 to keep the land free from 'all such filth and vice', continued to pour into the country through the ports. Another was the increasing availability of the Bible. The efforts of the clergy to ban the Scriptures were just as fruitless as their endeavours to ban good books. The more educated were being instructed and enlightened by the cultured writings of men like George Buchanan, whilst a remarkable impression was being made on the minds of ordinary people by pamphlets, plays, and ballads. Amongst the ballads, the most influential were those by the Wedderburn brothers. These included a catechism; the Ten Commandments in metre; some secular songs converted into religious poetry; twenty-two metrical psalms; and some hymns. One historian suggests that these ballads, which were set to popular tunes, did infinitely more to popularise Protestant views than the writings of the leading theologians could ever have done. Reformed preachers were being heard as well.

Many who fled the persecutions of Mary in England after the death of Edward VI in 1553 made their way to the continent, but some slipped over the border to Scotland. The first to come was William Harlow, a tailor from Edinburgh, who had been employed as a preacher during Edward's reign. After him came John Willock, who had been a chaplain to the Duke of Suffolk, the father of Lady Jane Grey. Willock had been sent to Scotland by the Duchess of East Friesland, ostensibly on a commercial mission to the Scottish court, but really to see 'what good work God would do by him in his native land.' And then they were joined by John Knox in the autumn of 1555.

Knox had set out secretly to visit the Protestants in Edinburgh and during his time there meetings were held in private houses. What he found encouraged him enormously. Writing to Elizabeth Bowes he commented, 'If I had not seen it with my eyes in my own country, I could not have believed it…The fervency here doth far exceed all others that I have seen…' A further encouragement was the response to Knox's appeal to them to separate themselves altogether from Roman Catholicism. In spite of their knowledge of the truth, the Protestants had continued to attend Roman Catholic worship and even to participate in the mass. Knox worked hard to show that such compromise was sinful. A debate was held on the subject in Edinburgh and Knox so skilfully answered the objections that had been raised against his views, that an agreement was reached to abstain from all further involvement in the mass. 'To argue with Knox', said one of those present, 'is like a foretaste of

Above and left: A section of the Reformers' Monument in Geneva which represents John Knox preaching to Nobility and politicians.

Judgement day. We see perfectly, that our shifts will serve nothing before God, seeing that they stand us in so small stead before man!'

Preaching tour

After spending some time in Edinburgh, Knox set out on a preaching tour that took him north into Angus, west into Ayrshire, and east again to Lothian—no small undertaking for a man on horseback, riding on rough, often almost impassable, tracks. The Lord's Supper was celebrated on several occasions, and everywhere he went, Knox found a hunger for the word of God. The clergy of course took alarm and Knox was summoned to appear before them in the church of the Black Friars on 15 May 1556 to answer charges of heresy. They clearly did not expect him to comply with the summons. When news reached their ears that he was actually on his way, they took fright and dropped the charges. This further time in Edinburgh was put to the same use as before. Writing to his mother-in-law, he observed, 'The trumpet blew the old sound three days together, till private houses…could not contain the voice of it. God for Christ his Son's sake grant me to be mindful that the sobs of my heart have not been in vain…Oh! Sweet were the death that should follow such forty days in Edinburgh, as here I have had three! Rejoice, Mother, the time of our deliverance approacheth; for as Satan rageth, so does the grace of the Holy Spirit abound, and daily giveth new testimonies of the everlasting love of our merciful Father.'

One blow that Knox did receive was the contemptuous dismissal by the Queen Mother, Mary of Lorraine, of a letter he wrote to her to try and persuade her to reform the church. By this time Mary of Lorraine was also Scotland's Regent. Her predecessor, the Earl of Arran, had been created Duke of Chatelherault and was now living in France. Knox was at pains to write in his most diplomatic style, but it was to no avail. When the letter was delivered to the Regent by the Earl of Glencairn, she merely glanced at it and then handed it to the Archbishop of Glasgow with a derogatory remark. Knox later published the letter with several sharp and spirited additions.

Around this time, Knox received letters from the English congregation in Geneva urging him to return and take up his

Left: Portrait of Mary of Lorraine (Guise) (1515-60) Queen of Scotland

Above: Knox letter to the Queen Regent

Above: Castle Campbell

duties as one of their pastors. Sending Marjory and Mrs Bowes—now a widow—ahead of him, he said his farewells to the believers, preaching to them in various places including Castle Campbell in Dollar. He finally left Scotland in July 1556, rejoined his family in Dieppe, and together they made their way to Geneva where, on 13 September 1556, they were received into the membership of the English church.

We can trace the workings of a wise providence in Knox's departure from Scotland at this time. Politically and spiritually, Scotland was not yet ready for a general reformation, and had Knox remained, the clergy would not have allowed him to live. As it was, when he left, they condemned him and had him burned in effigy at the cross of Edinburgh. By returning to Geneva when he did, his life was spared for future work in Scotland and in all likelihood, an outbreak of persecution against the Protestant noblemen was prevented.

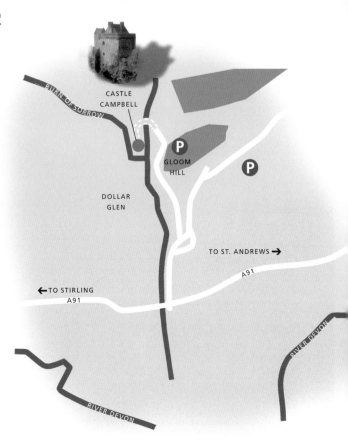

CASTLE CAMPBELL

BURN OF SORROW

P

GLOOM HILL

P

DOLLAR GLEN

TO ST. ANDREWS →

A91

← TO STIRLING
A91

RIVER DEVON

RIVER DEVON

Castle Campbell

Whether approaching on foot via a long winding icy path from below or driving up to the Castle's own car park, the appearance of Castle Campbell is sudden and forbidding.

Its sits isolated, high in the hills above Dollar around ten miles from Stirling.

The grassy mound on which it stands suggests that the site was used as a fortification from as early as the twelfth century.

Towards the end of the fifteenth century, the present tower house was built, replacing the fortified manor house destroyed by Walter Stewart. The then owner, Colin Campbell, first Earl of Argyll, renamed the building as Castle Campbell in 1489-90, after permission from King James IV was granted.

Distinguished guests to visit the Castle include Mary Queen of Scots in 1563, to celebrate the wedding of the fifth Earl's sister to James Stewart, Lord Doune and John Knox in 1566, where he preached and taught — having a most notable convert in the Earl .

In the nineteenth century, George Campbell, the sixth Duke of Argyll, sold the Castle and it fell further into ruin, until it came under the protection of the National Trust for Scotland in 1948.

TRAVEL DETAILS

Blackfriars St, Edinburgh

See map page 101

Castle Campbell Dollar

Dollar is situated 12 miles (20 kilometres) east of Stirling on the A91. The 15th century Castle Campbell is just outside the village, high up in Dollar Glen, and is clearly signposted. The castle is in the care of Historic Scotland. From April to September the castle is open every day from 0930–1830 hrs. From October to March, the castle is open on weekdays and Saturdays from 0930–1630 hrs. on Sundays from 1400–1630 hrs. but is closed both on Thursday afternoons and Fridays from December to March. ☎ 0131 668 8600 for further details. For details of bus services to Dollar, ☎ 01324 613777

Above, left: Blackfriars Street, Edinburgh. It was in the area of Blackfriars Street that the Church of the Blackfriars stood

Above: Stone marking the site of Cardinal Beaton's house at the corner of Blackfriars Street and the Cowgate

⑤ City of refuge

In Geneva, Knox and his little family found a community so at peace that he would love to have stayed there for the rest of his life, but letters from Scotland shattered his dream

The months that followed Knox's return to Geneva were probably the most peaceful in his life. He was happy in his family, happy in his congregation, happy in his friendships with the other city pastors and happy in Geneva itself. Writing to a friend, he confessed, 'In my heart I could have wished, yea, and cannot cease to wish, that it might please God to guide and conduct yourself to this place, where is the most perfect school of Christ that ever was in the earth since the days of the apostles. In other places I confess Christ to be truly preached; but manners and religion to be so sincerely reformed, I have not yet seen in any other place beside.' The Geneva of those days was a fine place for Christians to be, and under God it largely was what it was through the work and

Above and facing page: Wall of the Reformers (Monument de la Reformation Parc des Bastions. Conceived on a grand scale— it measures 325 ft (100 m) long and 30 ft (10 m) high—this monument, a phalanx of enormous granite statues, pays homage to the 16th-century religious movement spearheaded by William Farel, John Calvin, Theodore de Bèze, and John Knox. Their solemn 15-ft-tall likenesses are flanked by smaller statues of major Protestant figures, bas-reliefs, and inscriptions connected with the Reformation

Left: Autumn in the Parc des Bastions

ministry of its outstanding pastor, John Calvin.

Between Calvin and Knox a close friendship existed, though few details have been preserved. Knox was the elder of the two and had the deepest respect for Calvin. He referred to him as: 'That singular instrument of Christ Jesus in the glory of his gospel,' and acknowledged openly his indebtedness to him for: 'comfort, light and erudition.' We know little of Knox's home life here either. Marjory is described by Calvin as very charming, and in a letter to Knox after her death, he says of her: 'You found a wife the like of whom is not found everywhere.' During the Geneva years she bore Knox two sons, Nathaniel and Eleazar, and besides making a happy home for him, she was a help in his correspondence. Her mother lived with them as well.

The English congregation in Geneva had begun the previous November with about fifty members, but as other refugees drifted into the city, numbers eventually rose to over two hundred. Knox had the deepest affection for these men and women and could say that he would be content to end his days with them. In contrast to the situation in Frankfurt, the Geneva congregation were of one heart and mind as far as the ordering of worship was concerned. Their aim was not to have 'the face of an English church', but one simply in conformity with the word of God. That indeed was the ground rule. In the introduction to *The Form of Prayers and Ministration of the Sacraments* drawn up for the English congregation, the principle was laid down that everything in the Christian Church's confession, worship and discipline had to be determined by the teaching of the Bible. For this reason they believed that what was sung in public worship ought to be limited to the inspired words of the Psalms. Things that were merely matters of custom or tradition had no place.

The services themselves followed a straightforward

Geneva in the 16th Century

The Geneva of today is a city in Switzerland, but in the 16th century it was a small republic. By the time Calvin arrived in 1536 it had won its struggle for independence from the house of Savoy, had embraced the Reformation, and was by constitution an evangelical city. Surrounded by strong defensive walls it had the character of a fortress and was home to some ten thousand people, many of them refugees. In the old quarter of the modern Geneva there are streets still bearing the names that they had in Calvin's day. But though the private houses from that period are all gone, visitors are still able to visit St Peter's Church where Calvin preached, and the Temple de Nostre Dame la Neuve where Knox preached.

Above: Knox Chapel, Geneva

Right: Farel (Left) and Calvin in Geneva

pattern: confession of sin, the singing of a psalm, the prayer of invocation, the sermon followed by questions and discussion, the pastoral prayer, another psalm, and the benediction. There were no set prayers as there were in the English Prayer Book and the presiding minister was free to use his own. If there was to be a baptism it would take place at 'the common prayer and preaching'—that is, at a normal worship service in the presence of the congregation. The Lord's Supper was celebrated once a month or as often as the congregation determined. There was no kneeling, and the minister would sit at the table with the congregation, break the bread, give thanks and distribute it to all.

He would then do the same with the wine. Finally, after giving of thanks, the service would close with a psalm and a benediction.

Important visitors

Eight months after his return to Geneva, in May 1557, Knox received visitors from Scotland. They were James Syme and James Barron, both dear friends, and they had brought with them a letter signed by four of the Protestant noblemen. It declared that the believers whom Knox knew in Scotland were standing firm and had 'ane [one] godly thirst and desire, day by day', for his presence among them. 'If the Spirit of God will so move and permit time unto you', the noblemen wrote, 'we will heartily desire you, in the name of the Lord, that ye will return again to these parts, where ye shall find all faithful that ye left behind, not only glad to hear your doctrine, but will be ready to jeopard lives and goods in the forward-setting of the glory of God.' Earlier in the year, Knox had written to friends in Edinburgh and told them of the desire that he himself had to be in Scotland. It was his daily prayer in fact that he would not only be able to visit his native land but remain there. The call from Scotland, then, was not unwelcome. Nor was it disregarded. When he sought the advice of Calvin and his other colleagues in Geneva, they gave it as their opinion that he could not refuse such a call: 'Without declaring himself rebellious unto God and unmerciful to his country.' Since this was the conviction of his own heart also, he began to make preparations for his departure.

Knox arrived in Dieppe in October and found letters waiting for him from Scotland. But they were of a very different character from the one he had received in Geneva. It was all too apparent that there had been a change of heart. The enthusiasm of those who had been most anxious for him to return had considerably waned, with some regretting and others denying that they had had anything to do with the invitation.

Three days later a reply was on its way, addressed to the noblemen who had invited him to return. The text of it has been incorporated by Knox into his *History of the Reformation in Scotland*, and reveals both his heartache in leaving Geneva, and his awareness of the work these faint-hearted noblemen were obligated to do for the cause of Christ in Scotland. It was their duty to vindicate and deliver their subjects from all violence and oppression to the utmost of their power and not to leave the reformation of religion and the redress of wrongs simply to kings and clergy.

Knox sent off other letters and waited some time for replies. But hearing nothing, he eventually left Dieppe and made his way back to Geneva. His congregation had learned of what had happened and had re-elected him as one of their ministers. And so on his arrival in the spring of 1558 Knox was able to settle down again and resume his pastoral work.

The Godlie Band

In Scotland meanwhile things were changing for the better.

Above: The first Calvin College

Above: Ane Godlie Band

Knox's letters had reached their destination, and on 3 December 1557 a group of leading Protestant noblemen met in Edinburgh to consider what they ought to do. After careful deliberation they drew up and signed a *Godlie Band* [bond] *for maintenance of the Evangell*. '...Our duty well considered', they wrote, 'we do promise before the Majesty of God and His Congregation, that we by his grace, shall with all diligence continually apply our whole power, substance and our very lives to maintain, set forward and establish the most blessed word of God and His Congregation; and shall labour at our possibility to have faithful ministers purely and truly to minister Christ's Evangel and Sacraments to His people...' To achieve these ends, they resolved that the Scripture lessons and prayers from the English Prayer Book should be read every Sunday in the churches in which they had influence. They also agreed that the reformed preachers should teach in private houses only, until the government allowed them to do so in public; an agreement that led to some of the preachers becoming private chaplains to the nobles and exercising their ministries within the safety of the nobles' homes. Having made these resolutions they then renewed their invitation to Knox, writing at the same time to Calvin to ask him to use his influence to encourage Knox to accept. Because of the difficulties of finding a reliable messenger, however, almost a year was to elapse before these letters arrived in Geneva.

The First Blast of the Trumpet

After his return to Geneva in March 1558, one of the first things Knox did was to publish a book he had written during his months in Dieppe. It was entitled *The First Blast of the Trumpet against the Monstrous Regiment* [rule] *of Women*, and has achieved lasting notoriety. The opening sentence announced the theme: 'To promote a woman to bear rule, superiority, dominion, or empire, above any realm, nation, or city, is repugnant to nature, contumely [insulting] to God, a thing most contrarious to his revealed will and approved ordinance, and, finally, it is a subversion of all equity and justice.'

In developing his argument, Knox acknowledges that there are women whom God 'by singular privilege, and for certain causes known only to himself', has 'exempted from the common

Above and below: Knox's First Blast

Left: Portrait of Queen Elizabeth I (1533-1603) (oil on canvas) by John the Elder Bettes (fl.1531-76) (circle of)

rank.' Notwithstanding this: 'experience hath declared' that women in general lack 'the spirit of counsel and regiment', and ought not to be in positions of authority.

The subject of women bearing rule was one on which Knox had thought long and hard, and on which he had done a great deal of reading. He seems to have delayed putting pen to paper for some time, but with the situation in England worsening he felt unable to remain silent any longer. The cruel persecution by Queen Mary of England goaded him at last to action, and the *First Blast* is very much directed against her. In publishing it he fully anticipated a storm—and he was not disappointed. He was, 'curious, despiteful, a sower of sedition, and one day perchance be attainted for treason.' Nevertheless, Knox was so convinced of the truth of his

words and of the importance of them being heard that he had resolved to 'cover his eyes, and shut his ears' to the danger and the abuse.

The storm was not long in coming. One or two did speak up in Knox's defence, but for the most part, the reaction was decidedly adverse. A year after its publication Knox was forced to admit, 'My *First Blast* hath blown from me all my friends in England.' John Foxe, the martyrologist, complained to him on the bad taste of the publication and the severity of the language; he did so in a friendly manner; but many, who supported Queen Elizabeth when she came to the English throne later that year, raised an outcry against the book.

Elizabeth herself deeply resented the book and never forgave Knox for writing it. When Scotland needed England's help the following year, the Queen's anger over the *First Blast* made her very slow to respond. As for Knox, he never altered his views, but retained them to the last. Nevertheless, out of a desire to strengthen Elizabeth's authority because of her support for reformation, he did refrain from declaring them any further. He also held back from sounding a second and third blast as he had originally planned!

Criticism of the *First Blast* has certainly not died, and four hundred and fifty years after its publication, Knox continues to be vilified for it. We do well, however, to consider carefully what Thomas Carlyle, the 18th century historian and writer, once said of it: 'It is written with very great vehemency; the excuse for which, so far as it may really need excuse, is to be found in the fact that it was written while the fires of Smithfield were still blazing, on

hest [behest, command] of bloody Mary [Mary Tudor], and not long after Mary of Guise [Mary of Lorraine] had been raised to the regency of Scotland—maleficent [criminal] crowned women these two—covering poor England and poor Scotland with mere ruin and horror.' Carlyle went on to point out that Knox was no despiser of women. Quite the reverse in fact. His conduct toward them was full of respect, and in their sufferings and infirmities he showed great tenderness and helpfulness. His letters to Elizabeth Bowes are a fine illustration of that. It is worth noting too, that in Carlyle's opinion, the *First Blast* 'testifies to many high intellectual qualities in Knox, and especially to far more of learning than has ever been ascribed to him, or is anywhere else traceable in his writings.'

Above: *Renovated steam ship shuttles passengers back and forth along the length of Lake Lucerne*

Above: International Reformation Monument. From left to right, the four central figures are William Farel, John Calvin, John Théodore de Bèze, and John Knox. The group featured in the foreground offers a clue to the monument's size Below: Oliver Cromwell represented within the wall

Last days in Geneva

The final months of Knox's stay in Geneva, from March 1558 until January 1559, were busy ones. Not only did he have the ongoing care of the English congregation, but he was busy with his pen. We know, for instance, that he was involved in the production of a new translation of the Bible that was being prepared under the direction of William Whittingham, Knox's colleague in the ministry. This would be known as the *Geneva Bible*. Knox's involvement with it was both in the work of translation itself and in the preparation of accompanying notes for it.

We know, also, that Knox wrote a number of pamphlets during this period. These spell out clearly his views on civil government and of the rights of subjects against oppressive and idolatrous rulers. The nobles, he declared, had a right to remove a monarch who was oppressing his or her subjects and seeking to impose an idolatrous religion on them. Again, the common people had the right to demand the reformation of religion and to appoint faithful preachers for themselves if their rulers failed to

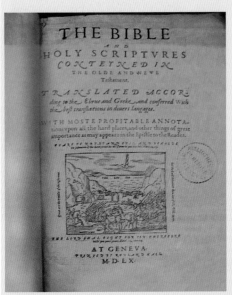

Above: First edition of of The Geneva Bible printed in Geneva

William Whittingham and the Geneva Bible

William Whittingham was born in 1524 and studied at Oxford University. Whilst travelling on the continent he embraced the Reformed faith and became one of its strongest supporters. Whittingham took Knox's side in the controversy at Frankfurt and subsequently followed him to Geneva. There he married the sister of John Calvin's wife, and was ordained to the ministry. Whittingham was Knox's colleague in the pastoral oversight of the English congregation in Geneva, but much of his time was spent in the translation of the *Geneva Bible*. He also wrote some metrical Psalms including an early version of the 23rd Psalm.

Whittingham returned to England in 1560 and was eventually made Dean of Durham. He died in 1579. Whittingham is best remembered as the leader of the team that produced the *Geneva Bible*, so called from the city where it was translated. The *Geneva Bible* was completed in 1560 and was mainly the work of three scholars, William Whittingham, Anthony Gilby and Thomas Sampson. It was also known as the 'Breeches Bible', from the rendering of Genesis 3:7, 'They sewed fig-leaves together and made themselves breeches.' The Geneva Bible was the first English Bible to be published with our complete chapter and verse division and was accompanied by explanatory notes from the pens of various Reformers. It became very popular and went through more than one hundred and thirty editions, the last in 1644. It was used by Reformers and Puritans, by the Pilgrim Fathers who sailed to America on the *Mayflower* in 1620, by Shakespeare, and by Oliver Cromwell in *The Soldier's Pocket Bible* that he issued to his troops in 1643. The *Geneva Bible* was also the first English Bible to be printed in Scotland and remained the preferred translation there long after the King James' Authorised Version came into use. Its popularity was well deserved for it was not only an excellent translation, relying significantly on the earlier work of William Tyndale, but very readable.

do so. It was also during these final months that Knox produced his most elaborate work, *The Doctrine of Predestination*. Extending to more than four hundred and fifty pages, it is the only theological treatise of any length that he published. It was written in reply 'to the cavillations [criticisms] of an adversary'—an Englishman by the name of Robert Cooke—and defends the doctrine both with clarity and caution.

The whole situation in England altered suddenly and dramatically, as the year 1558 drew to a close. On 17 November, Queen Mary died and was succeeded to the throne by her half-sister Elizabeth. This change in the monarchy was a source of great joy to the refugees and it was not long before they began to return from the continent. On 24 January 1559, the city council of Geneva gave permission to the members of the English congregation to depart, wishing them well. William Whittingham, on the congregation's behalf, expressed to the council the gratitude they felt for the welcome and hospitality they had received during their exile, and presented to the city, as a memorial of their names, the *Livre des Anglais* [The Book of the English].

By this time Knox had received the letters written to him from Scotland a year before, repeating the invitation to return. He spent Christmas with his family and congregation, and then, at the turn of the year, left Geneva for the last time and headed for Dieppe. Knox wanted to travel to Scotland through England so that he could visit his former congregations on the way, and had written to the English authorities asking for permission to do so. But when he arrived in Dieppe he found that not only had this permission been refused but that the bearers of his request had almost been thrown into prison. They had been accused of sympathising with Knox's highly unpopular views on female government. Knox wrote again, repeating his request for passage and though refused again, applied a third time. But he did not wait for an answer to this third request. He gave up on the plan to travel through England, found a boat that would take him straight to the port of Leith near Edinburgh, and landed there on 2 May 1559, determined, as one of his biographers has put it: 'That he would now blow the Lord's trumpet in his own homeland more earnestly and effectively than ever before.'

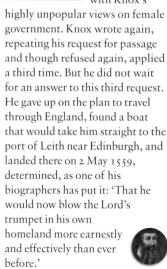

⑥ Victory!

Riots, siege, and civil war followed Knox's return to Scotland and for a time, the future of the reforming movement hung in the balance. But with history-making help from English troops the longed-for victory was finally achieved

Two months before Knox arrived in Scotland in 1559, a proclamation had been made at the market cross in Edinburgh by order of the Queen-Regent, Mary of Lorraine: no person was to preach or administer the sacraments without authority from the bishops. Throughout the previous year, the Queen-Regent had been surprisingly friendly toward the leading reformers. She had listened to their petitions for the reformation of religion and for protection from hostile clergy, and had given them various assurances. Some were so taken in by such expressions of goodwill that they even went so far as to rebuke those who 'appeared to suspect in her any venom of hypocrisy'. In the event, however, it was the ones who suspected a 'venom of hypocrisy' who were proved right. Mary had needed the support of the Protestant nobles for certain measures that she wished to carry through Parliament and she could not afford to antagonise them. However, as soon as she had achieved her goal, the mask was dropped and the Protestants saw her for the enemy of reformation

Above: *St Andrews Castle*

Facing page: *Church of the Holy Rude, St John Street, Stirling*

that she had always been. When the Earl of Glencairn and Sir Hugh Campbell sought to reason with her and urge the fulfilment of the assurances she had given, her haughty reply was, 'It becometh not subjects to burden their princes with promises further than it pleaseth them to keep the same.'

The March proclamation was ignored by four of the reformed preachers, Paul Methven, John Christison, William Harlow, and John Willock. They were summoned to stand trial before the Court of Justiciary in Stirling on 10 May. It was at this critical moment that Knox arrived in Scotland, and as soon as he heard about the summons, he determined to accompany the preachers to Stirling—so also did a large contingency of supporters from Dundee and Angus. They made their way to Perth (known then as St Johnestoun), and from there, John Erskine, the Laird of Dun, was sent to Stirling to assure the Queen-Regent that they came unarmed and simply in support of their ministers. Mary sent Erskine back, authorising him to promise in her name that the trial would not go ahead; believing her, he undertook to persuade the men to return to their homes. But the Regent's double-dealing was not long in coming to light. When May 10 came and no preachers appeared in Stirling, the four men were immediately outlawed. All persons were prohibited, under pain of being treated as rebels, from harbouring or assisting them.

Riot in Perth

The news reached Perth the following day, and Knox preached a powerful sermon in St John's Kirk against broken faith, lies, deceit, and the idolatry of the mass. It was to have unexpected consequences. When the sermon was over, a priest, in defiance of what had been preached, began to celebrate mass. A boy who observed him protested and the priest struck him. The boy then threw a stone at the priest, which missed him but smashed an image. The result was uproar. In a few moments the altar, images, and ornaments had all been torn down and trampled under foot. The noise attracted others, who, in spite of the appeals of the magistrates and preachers, attacked the monasteries of the Black and Grey Friars and the

Above: St John's Kirk, Perth where Knox preached a powerful sermon with unexpected results in May 1559

Above: Blackfriars Chapel, St Andrews, the one remaining fragment of a Dominican Friary which was attacked on 14 June 1559

magnificent Charterhouse of the Carthusian monks—reducing them all to ruins. The destruction then spread to other places and in the space of a few weeks, the houses of the monks in St Andrews, Crail, Cupar, Stirling, Linlithgow, Edinburgh, and Glasgow, suffered the same fate.

For all this destruction it is quite unjust to blame John Knox. In the Perth case, the destruction of the monasteries was an unpremeditated act, carried out by people whom Knox termed 'the rascal multitude', and in the face of earnest appeals. A similar thing happened with the Abbey of Scone. Knox tells us that, 'men of the greatest estimation laboured with all diligence for the safety of it'; but it was destroyed nevertheless by people looking for loot. Such behaviour was prejudicial to the movement for reform and there is no evidence that Knox or any of the other preachers ever gave any

encouragement to it. As for the churches, we know that when the Cathedral of Dunkeld was to be purged the following year of everything associated with Catholicism, strict instructions were given that 'neither the desks, windows, nor doors be anywise burnt or broken, either glass-work or iron-work'. And that would have been typical. The Reformers were happy to put these pre-Reformation churches to use as places of Protestant worship and had no interest in their destruction.

When news of the Perth riots reached the Regent's ears, she was so enraged that she vowed to utterly destroy Perth, 'man, woman, and child, and to consume the same by fire, and thereafter to salt it, in sign of a perpetual desolation.' But the Protestant nobles were swift to take action to prevent her. When their explanations and their disavowals of rebellion all fell on deaf ears, and the Regent's French troops were advancing toward the town, they raised an army against them of such strength that the Regent was forced to come to terms. An agreement was reached by which the Protestant forces would withdraw from Perth on conditions that the Regent accepted. But as had happened so often before, her promises were shamefully broken, and there was great suffering in Perth as a result. It weakened the Regent's hands considerably. Such was the feeling of revulsion at her conduct that many noblemen who had been loyal to her before, now identified themselves fully with the reformers. Amongst these were Lord James Stewart and the Earl of Argyl; Stewart was a man who in coming days would do much for the Christian good of Scotland.

Powerful preaching in St Andrews

The nobles who were promoting the cause of reform had come to be known as the Lords of the Congregation—the Congregation being the name adopted by those who had broken with the old Catholic religion. On 30 May, these Lords of the Congregation entered into another solemn bond: 'faithfully promising to assist and defend one another against all persons that would pursue them for religion's sake.' They resolved to effect reformation in all the places where they had authority and where the majority of the people were in favour of it—abolishing Catholicism and establishing Protestant worship. The place chosen for this work to begin was St Andrews, where Lord James Stewart was Prior of the Abbey; it was arranged that Knox should come and preach.

Above: 'Knox preaching at St Andrews to the Lords of the Congregation on 11 June 1559' by Sir David Wilkie, R.A.

Left: St Andrews
Cathedral. The
cathedral was stripped
at this time of
everything associated
with Roman
Catholicism, and was
then abandoned as a
place of worship in
preference to the parish
church. It rapidly fell
into decay, with much
of its stone being taken
for building elsewhere

Knox arrived on 9 June, having preached in the Fife coast villages of Anstruther and Crail on the way. A warning was waiting for him. The Archbishop of St Andrews had sent a message saying that if: 'John Knox presented himself at the preaching-place in his town and principal church, he should make him be saluted with a dozen of culverings [muskets], whereof the most part would light upon his nose.' Knox's friends were alarmed at this and tried to dissuade him from preaching. But he was determined: 'As for the fear of danger that may come to me let no man be solicitous, for my life is in the custody of Him whose glory I seek, and therefore I cannot so fear their boast or tyranny that I

will cease from doing my duty, when of His mercy He offereth me the occasion. I desire the hand or weapon of no man to defend me. I only crave audience, which if it be denied me here I must seek further where I may have it.'

Sunday 11 June found Knox in the pulpit of the Parish Church, preaching from the account in the Gospels of the ejection of the buyers and sellers from the Temple! No one interrupted him, and his audience—which was vast and included many scholars from the university—responded positively. During the previous week there had been little enthusiasm in St Andrews for reformation, but after Knox's sermon on the Sunday, and the sermons of the four following days, the majority of the people and not a few of the clergy renounced their allegiance to Catholicism. This was just the beginning. Over the course of the next few months, the example of St Andrews was followed by many others. In a letter written on 2 September for example, Knox says, 'I have been in continual travel…and notwithstanding the fevers have vexed me the space of a month, yet have I travelled through the most part of this realm where, all praise be to his blessed Majesty, men of all sorts and conditions embrace the truth… So that the trumpet soundeth all over, blessed be our God.'

Civil war

In all her double-dealing with the reformers, the Queen Regent had had a very clear objective in mind. She wanted to subject Scotland politically to the authority of France. Back in 1558, when with parliamentary consent her sixteen-year-old daughter Mary married Francis, the heir to the French throne, two treaties were drawn up, one public, the other secret. By the public treaty Scotland was to remain an independent country. By the secret one, which the Queen Regent signed, the King of France was to become King of Scotland if Mary should die without leaving an heir. Meanwhile, there was a growing French presence in Scotland. Frenchmen held many of the chief positions in government, and to reinforce the Regent's authority, more and more French troops were entering the country. If the Regent was allowed to have her way, Scotland would soon become part of France, the authority of the Church of Rome would be fully restored, and Protestantism would be crushed out of existence. But the Lords of the Congregation were determined that Mary should *not* have her way, and in this they had the support of a growing number of the Scottish people. Protestantism was gaining ground, the presence and activities of the French were being increasingly resented, and there was a sense of outrage at the Regent's double dealing and at her high-handed attempts to stamp out the Reformation and undermine the nation's liberties. The result was a civil war that lasted until July 1560.

Knox's political views

Knox believed that no one has an inherent right to rule over others, and that all rulers, including monarchs, are invested with their authority for the public good and that they are subject to civil law. If they govern contrary to the laws of God or in such a way as violates the welfare of the people, Knox believed that it is not treason or rebellion to oppose them and to replace them by those more fitted to rule. He gave expression to such views in sermons, pamphlets, and debates, and they had an enormous influence on the policies adopted at this critical time in Scotland's history.

Above: Church of the Holy Rude, St John Street, Stirling

Darkness before the dawn

It was a difficult task that confronted the Congregation. A large body of French troops was occupying the strategically important port of Leith, and its defences were strong. Several attempts at a siege were made but with each one ending in defeat, the courage of the Protestant forces began to wane. Many fled the city. Finally, on 5 November, the French troops themselves mounted an attack and in the engagement, inflicted such defeat that the morale of those remaining was broken. In fear and despair they retreated to Stirling. It was their darkest hour.

Knox had been with them in Edinburgh, preaching to them in St Giles, seeking to sustain their courage, and he went with them now to Stirling. There, in the Church of the Holy Rude, he preached one of the most influential sermons of his life; a sermon that has been described as marking a turning point in the history of the Reformation.

Taking as his text Psalm 80: 4–8, he dismissed the idea that God was angry with them for having taken up the sword of self-defence. It was because of their *sins* that God was withholding his blessing; and after some very pointed application of this to his

Above: Knox's secret mission to England took him to the castle of Berwick-upon-Tweed. The few remains of the castle lie just beyond the railway viaduct. The ruins extend up the steep bank to the railway station. The Royal Border Bridge (pictured) was built 1847–50 by Robert Stephenson. It has 28 arches and the height is 126 ft and carries the railway across the Tweed

hearers and calls to repentance, a note of strong encouragement was struck. God often permitted the wicked to triumph for a while, and exposed his chosen people to mockery, dangers, and apparent destruction, in order to humble them, and make them look to him for deliverance and victory. If then they turned in all sincerity to God, Knox was in no doubt that their present distress would be followed by success. It was God's eternal truth for which they stood, and though that truth might be oppressed for a time, it would ultimately triumph.

The sermon had a powerful effect on Knox's hearers. They had come into church in deep despondency, with hopes well nigh extinguished. But now their depression was gone. Hope had been rekindled. God was on their side and victory would be theirs. It is a fine illustration of what Thomas Randolph, Queen Elizabeth's envoy to Scotland, said of Knox in one of his dispatches, 'The voice of one man is able in one hour to put more life in us than five hundred trumpets continually blustering in our ears.'

Making common cause

For some time the nobles had been appealing for aid from England. Knox himself for a time was at the centre of these negotiations, adding to his other labours that of a diplomat. At one point he even undertook a secret mission to England, and he was in frequent correspondence over the matter.

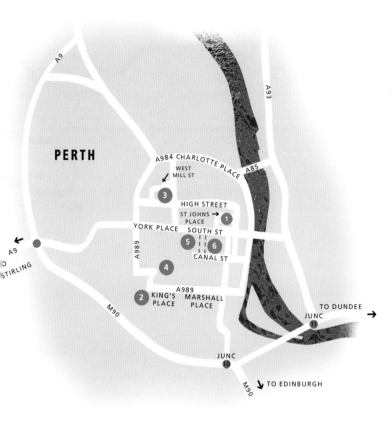

KEY TO PLACES

1   ST JOHN'S KIRK, ST JOHN'S PLACE

2   RAILWAY STATION, LEONARD STREET

3   TOURIST INFORMATION CENTRE, WEST MILL STREET

4   BUS STATION, LEONARD STREET

5   THERE ARE PUBLIC TOILETS IN A LANE OFF SOUTH STREET

6   PARKING IS AVAILABLE IN CANAL STREET AND IN VARIOUS
    OTHER PARTS OF THE CITY CENTRE

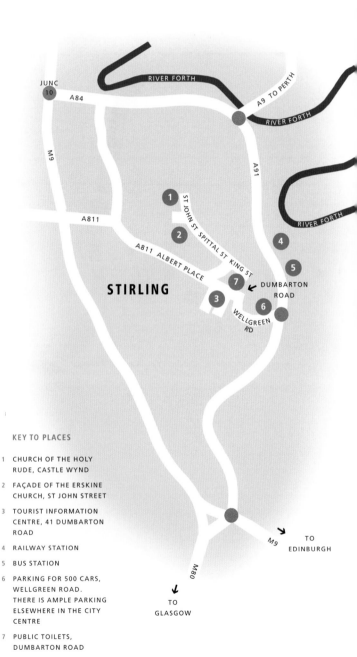

KEY TO PLACES

1 CHURCH OF THE HOLY RUDE, CASTLE WYND

2 FAÇADE OF THE ERSKINE CHURCH, ST JOHN STREET

3 TOURIST INFORMATION CENTRE, 41 DUMBARTON ROAD

4 RAILWAY STATION

5 BUS STATION

6 PARKING FOR 500 CARS, WELLGREEN ROAD. THERE IS AMPLE PARKING ELSEWHERE IN THE CITY CENTRE

7 PUBLIC TOILETS, DUMBARTON ROAD

Above: *Stirling Castle*

This all meant long days for him—he says in one of his letters, 'in twenty-four hours, I have not had four free to natural rest'. It also meant that he was in constant danger—'I have need of a good and an assured horse for great watch is laid for my apprehension, and large money promised to any that shall kill me.'

It took a long time and much effort to persuade Queen Elizabeth that it was in England's best interest to come to Scotland's aid. And it *was* in England's best interests. France not only had designs on Scotland; it was looking forward to the day when the Regent's daughter, the young Queen Mary, would be queen of France, Scotland and England. If Elizabeth valued her throne and England's independence she needed to act. At last the prevaricating ended. On 27 February 1560, a treaty was signed in which she committed herself to assist in expelling the French forces by sending an army into

Scotland. It was urgently needed. After a French victory at Kinghorn in Fife, the Regent had sneeringly remarked, 'Where is now John Knox's God? My God is now stronger than his, yea in Fife.' But the end was drawing near. On 4 April thousands of English and Scots soldiers joined forces—a notable event after centuries of conflict—and two days later the siege of Leith was renewed.

It took three months for the siege to end, and when it did, it was not because the Leith defences had been breached. The inefficient soldiers of the Scots and English armies had been no match for the French. But other things had happened to hasten peace—the death of the Queen-Regent in early June, the eventual resolution of Queen Elizabeth to prosecute the war with vigour, the blocking of the Firth of Forth by an English fleet, and certain events in France. On 16 June, commissioners from England and France met to conclude negotiations, and on

Above: St Andrews Cathedral, St Rules Tower

6 July, the Treaty of Edinburgh was signed. French and English troops were to leave Scotland; the fortifications of Leith were to be destroyed; an amnesty was to be granted to all who had been involved in resisting the Regent; and the Scottish Parliament was to meet to settle the affairs of the kingdom. On 15 July, ten thousand French troops set sail for France, mostly on English ships. And then on Sunday 19, the Congregation assembled in St Giles' Church to give thanks to God for the restoration of peace, and the success that had crowned their endeavours.

The Reformation settlement

When the Scottish Parliament began its historic sittings on the first of August, the subject of religion dominated. A petition was presented by a number of Protestants in which Parliament was requested to use its power for the reformation of the church. In response, it instructed the ministers to draw up a Confession of Faith, outlining 'the doctrine which they would maintain as wholesome and true', and which they wished Parliament to establish as the religion of Scotland. The work was entrusted to six men, each by coincidence with the same forename—John Knox, John Spottiswoode, John Row, John Willock, John Douglas, and John Winram. In the remarkably short space of four days the confession was ready to be presented to Parliament. It was divided into twenty-five brief chapters, and contained statements on key matters such as God, the creation of man, original sin, the incarnation of Christ, election, the death, burial, resurrection, and ascension of Christ, the marks of a true church, and the proper administration of the sacraments. The chapters were read over carefully one by one to the members of Parliament and on 17 August 1560, the Confession was accepted and ratified by an overwhelming majority.

Finally, on 24 August, Acts were passed abolishing the jurisdiction of the Pope in Scotland, prohibiting the celebration of the mass, and repealing all the laws that had been made in support of the Roman Catholic Church, and against the Reformed faith. Scotland's religion, at least officially, was now firmly Protestant and evangelical.

Above: *The ruin of Blackfriars Chapel photographed in the early 1870s*

TRAVEL DETAILS

1. Perth
Travel

At one time Perth was Scotland's capital city. It lies approximately 42 miles (68 kilometres) north of Edinburgh and 21 miles (34 kilometres) west of Dundee. There are excellent road and rail connections to it. Visitors driving north from Edinburgh should leave the M90 at junction 10, those driving west from Dundee at junction 11. For details of train services to Perth, ☎ National Rail 08457 484950 For details of City Link bus services, ☎ 08705 505050

St John's Kirk

The 12th century St John's Kirk is

situated on St John's Place and is open Monday to Saturday, 10am till 4pm. The bell that is rung today is the same one that Knox would have heard. It dates from 1506. In 1926 a new pulpit was installed, modelled on the pulpit Knox preached from in St Andrews. For many years the east part of the church was known as the John Knox Chapel.

Tourist Information

The Tourist Information Centre is situated on Lower City Mills, West Mill Street. ☎ 01738 450600

2. St Andrews

For street map and for tourist and travel information see details at the close of Chapters 1 and 2.

Blackfriars Chapel

This one remaining part of what was once a Dominican Friary is situated on South Street and can be viewed from the pavement.

The Cathedral

Like St Rule's Tower the Cathedral dates from the 12th century. It is in the care of Historic Scotland and is open daily.

Church of the Holy Rude

The Church of the Holy Rude

The Church of the Holy Rude, Stirling's principal church for more than 500 years, is situated on Castle Wynd and is open daily 10am–5pm, 1 May–20 September.

Stirling Tour

During summer months an open top Heritage Bus Tour operates with a guided commentary on places of historic interest For details, ☎ 01786 475019/479901

Tourist Information

The Tourist Information Centre is situated on Dumbarton Road.
☎ 01786 475019

Admission to the grounds is free but there is a charge for the Cathedral Museum. ☎ 01334 472563 for further details.

3. Stirling

The Royal Burgh of Stirling lies approximately 35 miles (57 kilometres) northwest of Edinburgh. Visitors travelling by car should leave the M9 at either junction 9 or 10. Stirling is also readily accessible by rail. For train times, ☎ National Rail, 08457 484950. For details of City Link bus services to Stirling, ☎ 08705 505050.

Above: James Guthrie, c.1612–61. Guthrie was one of the ministers of the Holy Rude from 1649–61. During the Covenanting struggle for the freedom of the Scottish Church from royal control, Guthrie suffered martyrdom

Below: The founding ministers of the Secession Church. Ebenezer Erskine, seated on the left, was one of the ministers of the Holy Rude until his suspension from the ministry in 1733

Above: *Façade of the Erskine Church, St John Street, Stirling. The Church of the Holy Rude had long been divided into two parts, East and West. In spite of his suspension, Erskine continued to preach in the West part until 1740 when he was finally deposed from the ministry of the Church of Scotland. A new church for his congregation was completed in 1742 and Erskine remained minister there until his death in 1754. The church was replaced by another on the same site in 1826. Only its façade remains, which has been incorporated into a modern youth hostel. In the foreground of the picture is an elaborate monument to Erskine, erected over his tomb in 1859.*

3. Berwick-upon-Tweed

For street map and for tourist and travel information see details at the end of Chapter 2

Berwick-upon-Tweed Castle

Dating from the 13th to the 16th century, Berwick castle is open at any reasonable time.

Little is left of the ancient castle, except for a small ruin of the watch-tower on the riverside near the railway bridge and a length of wall which guarded a flight of steps up the steep bank. Much of the castle stone went into the railway bridge and the station occupies the castle site.

❼ A fearless preacher

For most of the last twelve years of his life John Knox lived in Edinburgh. There he had several of his famous encounters with Mary, Queen of Scots, and was accused by her of treason. Knox also provoked the Queen's displeasure when after three years as a widower, he married Margaret Stewart—a distant relative of the Queen herself!

Since the July of the previous year, Knox had been the minister of St Giles, but on account of the dangers arising from the civil war, and the need that there was for him in other places, he had only preached there occasionally. With the conflict now at an end he was able to settle into a more regular pattern of ministry. He preached twice every Sunday and three times during the week. There was a weekly meeting with the elders of the church, a weekly meeting with other ministers, and time spent in study every day. In addition, Knox was often preaching elsewhere in Scotland, something that meant long journeys on horseback. In his poor health it all proved too exhausting, and a decision was taken to call John Craig, the minister of the Canongate in Edinburgh, to assist him. Craig was a Scotsman who had been converted on the continent through reading a copy of John Calvin's *Institutes of the Christian Religion*, which he had found in a Roman Catholic library. Returning to Scotland in 1560, he preached for a short time

Above: John Knox house around 1760. To the right is the Netherbow Port, originally one of the principal gates of the city

Facing page: John Knox's House today

in the Magdalen Chapel before being appointed minister of the Canongate. Though chosen as Knox's colleague in 1562 it was not until the following year that he was able to take up his responsibilities.

As many as three thousand people, both rich and poor, would gather to listen to Knox preaching in St Giles. It is a matter of regret that we have a complete text of only one of Knox's sermons. It dates from 1565, and he had preached a sermon on Isaiah 26:13–21. Lord Darnley, who had married the recently widowed Mary, Queen of Scots, took great offence at it. The result was a summons to appear before the Privy Council and a prohibition from preaching when the Queen and her husband were in residence in Edinburgh. In his own defence, Knox published the controversial sermon and it remains the only complete example of his pulpit work that has survived. Commenting on it, one of Knox's biographers says, 'It gives evidence of considerable scholarship, of immense familiarity with Scripture, of good acquaintance with ancient history, and of great fervour of spirit.' Doubtless, the same would have been true of all his sermons.

Knox's preaching was also marked by plainness of speech and great courage. He once declared that, 'From Isaiah, Jeremiah, and other inspired writers, he had learned to call a fig a fig, and a spade a spade.' On another occasion, in one of his famous interviews with Queen Mary, he could say, 'Without [outside] the preaching place, Madam, I think few have occasion to be offended at me. There, Madam, I am not master of myself, but must obey Him who commands me to speak plain, and to flatter no flesh upon the face of the earth.' At the root

Left: Part of a plan of Edinburgh, 1573. The wide street in the centre is the High Street leading from the Castle on the west by St Giles' church, the Cross, and the Tron Church to John Knox's House and the Nether Bow Port on the east

Facing page: The Palace of Holyroodhouse

of it all was what he once described as, 'A reverential fear of my God.' Its effect was to make him say whatever God put in his mouth: 'without any respect of persons.'

The First Book of Discipline

Returning to the period immediately following the Reformation settlement of 1560, we find Knox not only preaching constantly, but busy with his pen as well. In particular, he was involved, with some other ministers, in drawing up one of the great documents of the Scottish Church, *The First Book of Discipline*. This sets out in detail

the vision these men had for a thoroughly reformed church. It addressed itself to such things as the proper administration of the sacraments, the election of gospel ministers, their qualifications and duties, the provision to be made for their support, the process of ecclesiastical discipline, the appointment of elders and deacons, the care of the poor, the ordinance of marriage, and the burial of the dead.

However, the *Book of Discipline*, was not confined to church matters. The whole of Chapter VII is taken up with Knox's plan for a system of national education. He argued that every church should have a schoolmaster who could teach the children grammar and Latin; every major town should have a college or grammar school; and in St Andrews, Glasgow, and Aberdeen there should be a university. For the good of both

Above: The Magdalen Chapel. Dating from 1541, the Magdalen Chapel lies on the Cowgate between Candlemaker Row and George IV Bridge. It was in the Magdalen Chapel that the first General Assembly of the reformed church's leaders took place in December 1560

the children themselves and the nation as a whole, education should be compulsory. In the case of children whose parents were too poor to afford an education, it should be provided at the state's expense. Sadly, the book never received the level of support from the nobles and rulers that was needed for its full implementation.

Knox's early days in Edinburgh were overshadowed by a painful personal trial. Toward the end of December 1560, his wife Marjory died at the young age of about twenty-seven. In his will, Knox refers to her as 'my late dearest spouse...of blessed memory', and bequeaths to his sons the same

benediction, 'their dearest mother' had left them, namely, 'that God, for His Son Christ Jesus' sake, would, of His mercy, make them His true fearers and as upright worshippers of Him as any that ever sprang out of Abraham's loins.' At the time of Marjory's death these boys were very young but Knox would at least have had the assistance of their grandmother, Mrs Bowes, who had remained a member of the household.

Mary, Queen of Scots

There were clouds, too, on the national horizon. The young Queen Mary and her husband, the King of France, had refused to ratify the Treaty of Leith and had in fact made preparations for an invasion of Scotland. This never took place because on 5 December 1560, the French King died. But there was further trouble ahead. On 19 August 1561, the young widow of Francis II, Mary Queen of Scots, arrived in Scotland. And as her letters and subsequent actions make clear, one of her principal aims was the restoration of the Roman Catholic religion.

Mary was nineteen years of age at the time, tall, beautiful, very intelligent, with winning manners and a forceful personality. She had spent most of her life in France, and it seems to have been with no great joy that she returned to the land of her birth. According to a report from Paris at the time: 'The miserable young woman is said to have wept both day and night. And no wonder since she was being deported from such delights to a horrid and rough island, and to a

Top: *St Giles' Church*

Above: *The pulpit from which Knox preached in St Giles. It is located in the Museum of Scotland, Chambers Street*

people unappreciative of her, and dissenting from her in religion.' Many of the Scottish people, however, were not so unappreciative as the reporter

supposes, nor so unsympathetic toward Mary's religion. Roman Catholicism still had a great deal of grass-roots support in Scotland, whilst even amongst the Protestants there were many who were enthusiastic in their welcome of the young Queen. But others— including Knox—had the gravest misgivings about Mary's coming, and, as events were to prove, with ample justification.

The trouble began almost immediately. On the Sunday after Mary's arrival she gave orders for mass to be celebrated in the chapel of the Palace of Holyroodhouse.

This was in clear defiance of the 1560 Act of Parliament that forbade the celebration of mass. When they heard about it, the Lairds of Fife were so enraged that only the presence of Lord James Stewart at the chapel door prevented them from breaking up the service. There were widespread feelings of anger and alarm. Knox himself privately counselled calm, but on the following Sunday, from the pulpit of St Giles, he thundered against the mass, saying, 'One mass is more fearful to me than if ten thousand enemies were landed in any part of the realm of purpose to suppress the whole religion.' For these early Protestants, the reintroduction of the mass was not only the first step toward the restoration of a religion that had enshrouded the land in spiritual darkness, but it was the herald of oppression, banishment, imprisonments, torture and death. The civil and religious liberties of the nation, dearly won, were under serious threat again. It is true that after 1560 the mass was prohibited by law under the penalty of death, though no one ever suffered that penalty in Scotland. No one suffered after the Reformation as the Protestants had suffered before it.

Shortly after his sermon in St Giles, Knox was summoned to appear before Queen Mary.

What followed was the first of their famous interviews, detailed summaries of which Knox has given us in his *History of the Reformation in Scotland*. In this first encounter, which took place in the presence of Lord James Stewart, Mary accused him among other things of writing a book against her rightful authority, *The First Blast of the Trumpet*. In his reply, Knox assured her that the *First Blast* was written not against her but 'most especially against that wicked Jezebel of England' [Mary Tudor,

Bloody Mary]. He himself would be as content to live under her reign as the Apostle Paul was to live under Nero; and if she abstained from persecuting the saints she would have nothing to fear either from him or his book.

Later in the interview, Mary raised with him the subject of disobedience to rulers: 'Think ye that subjects, having the power, may resist their princes?'. Bold Knox responded: 'If their princes exceed their bounds, Madam, no doubt they may be resisted, even by power. For there is neither greater honour, nor greater obedience, to be given to kings or princes, than God hath commanded to be given unto father and mother. But the father may be stricken with a frenzy, in which he would slay his children. If the children arise, join themselves together, apprehend the father, take the sword from him, bind his hands, and keep him in prison till his frenzy be overpast—think ye, Madam, that the children do any wrong? It is even so, Madam, with princes that would murder the children of God that are subjects unto them. Their blind zeal is nothing but a mad frenzy, and therefore, to take the sword from them, to bind their hands, and to cast them into prison, till they be brought to a more sober mind, is no disobedience against princes, but just obedience, because it agreeth with the will of God.' Knox's reply silenced the Queen for more than a quarter of an hour!

Turning finally to the subject of religion, the Queen declared that she would, 'defend the Kirk of Rome', for it was, she thought, 'the true Kirk of God'. In reply, Knox said, 'Your *will*, Madam, is no

Left: Portrait of Mary
Queen of Scots (1542–87)
(oil on panel) by Scottish
school (16th century)

Facing page: Knox
preaching in St Giles

reason; neither doth your *thought* make that Roman harlot to be the true and immaculate spouse of Jesus Christ.' It was strong language, he knew, but he could defend it: 'Wonder not, Madam, that I call Rome an harlot; for that church is altogether polluted with all kind of spiritual fornication, as well in doctrine as in manners.' Feeling that she was getting out of her depth Mary said to him, 'If they were here whom I have heard, they would answer you.' Knox wished that they were: 'Madam, would to God that the learnedest Papist in Europe, and he that ye would best believe, were present with Your Grace to sustain the argument; and that ye would patiently abide to hear the matter reasoned to the end! Then, I doubt not, Madam, but ye should hear the vanity of the Papistical Religion, and how small ground it hath within the Word of God.' But Knox knew that they would never come 'to have the ground of their religion searched out' because, 'They know that they are never able to sustain an argument, except fire and sword and their own laws be judges.'

The encounter ended shortly after with the Queen being called to dinner. As he left, Knox said to her, 'I pray God, Madam, that ye may be as blessed within the Commonwealth of Scotland, if it be the pleasure of God, as ever Deborah was in the Commonwealth of Israel.' But in his heart he feared the worst. On being asked what he thought of the Queen, he replied quite candidly: 'If there be not in her a proud mind, a crafty wit, and an indurate [hard] heart against God and His truth, my judgment faileth me.'

A queen in tears

In the summer of 1563, Knox learned of negotiations that had been taking place for the marriage of the Queen to Don Carlos, son of Philip II of Spain. Justly fearing for the future of Protestantism in Scotland if such a marriage were to take place, since Don Carlos was a Roman Catholic, he spoke out against it in one of his sermons. The Queen was enraged. Summoning Knox to her presence she demanded with tears: 'What have you to do with my marriage? Or what are *you* within this Commonwealth?' To this Knox replied that he was: 'A subject born within the same, Madam. And albeit I be neither Earl, Lord, nor baron within it, yet hath God made me—how abject so ever I be in your eyes—a profitable member within the same. Yea, Madam, to me it appertains no less to forewarn of such things as may hurt it, if I foresee them, than it doth to any of the nobility; for both my vocation and my conscience crave plainness of me. Therefore, Madam, to yourself I say that which I spake in public place: Whensoever the nobility of this realm shall consent that ye be subject to an unfaithful husband, they do as much as in them lieth to renounce Christ, to banish truth from them, to betray the freedom of this realm, and perchance they shall in the end do small comfort to yourself.'

More tears followed from Mary, during which Knox stood still, 'without any alteration of countenance for a long season.' But it was not because he was cold and stonyhearted as is so often alleged. Far from it. 'Madam', he eventually responded, 'in God's presence I speak. I never delighted in the weeping of any of God's creatures. Yea, I can scarcely well abide the tears of my own boys when my own hand correcteth; much less can I rejoice in Your Majesty's weeping. But, seeing I have offered to you no just occasion to be offended, but have spoken the truth, as my vocation craves of me, I must sustain, albeit unwillingly, Your Majesty's tears, rather than I dare hurt my conscience, or betray my Commonwealth through my silence.'

A charge of treason

It was faithfulness at a price. These encounters made him an object of hatred to Queen Mary, who vowed to God that she would be revenged. Later that year she came close to achieving her goal. Writing a letter to the Protestant leaders, she urged them to come to Edinburgh for consultation on the trial of two men who had been arrested for disturbing a mass at Holyrood and seized the opportunity of charging Knox with treason. He was brought before the Queen and an assembly of Privy Councillors, and there he defended himself so ably that to the Queen's embarrassment he was acquitted. 'That night', says Knox, 'was neither dancing nor fiddling in the Court, for Madam was disappointed of her purpose, which was to have had John Knox in her will by vote of her nobility.'

But the Queen and her actions were not the Reformer's only source of anxiety at this time. A number of the Protestant nobles

Above: Mary, Queen of Scots, in tears when Knox condemned her proposed marriage to Philip II of Spain

were seemingly blind to the danger that Mary posed to Scotland's religious freedom, and increasingly resented the things Knox was saying. There were open disagreements over the negotiations for Mary's marriage. Some of the nobles were actually in favour of it, believing that Protestantism would come to no harm. Knox for his part did not shrink from plain speaking in his dealings with these men, and the result was tension and alienation. Between Knox and Lord James Stewart there was a breach of friendship which lasted for over a year. Another prominent nobleman, Maitland of Lethington, became his open opponent.

For Knox, however, there was one situation in these troubled times that did change for the better. In March 1554, after he had spent three lonely years as a widower, he remarried.

His bride was Margaret Stewart, daughter of Lord Ochiltree, a young woman much his junior. She was only about seventeen whilst he was about fifty. His Roman Catholic opponents accused him of using the dark arts to secure her hand. One wrote, 'As is plainly reported in the country, he did so allure that poor gentlewoman by sorcery and witchcraft that she could not live without him.' Queen Mary was very angry since Margaret Stewart was a distant relative of hers! For Knox it meant happiness and companionship again, and their marriage brightened his final years. Margaret was a very devoted and attentive wife and they had three daughters, Martha, Margaret, and Elizabeth who married the famous minister of Ayr, the Revd John Welsh.

TRAVEL DETAILS

Edinburgh Travel

For details of train services to Edinburgh, ☎ National Rail, 08457 484950 or Traveline, 0131 225 3858
For information on bus and coach services, ☎ Traveline, 0131 225 3858
For Edinburgh Airport, ☎ 0131 333 1000

Above: *The Palace of Holyroodhouse*

St Giles' Cathedral

Situated on the High Street/Royal Mile just down from George IV Bridge, this ancient church is open daily. ☎ 0131 225 9442 for details.

John Knox House

A short distance down the High Street/Royal Mile from St Giles where Knox preached is the mediaeval town house where he lived. In the 16th century one of the principal gates of the city, the Nether Bow Port, stood immediately to the east of the house, whilst to the west, in the direction of the castle, lay the market cross and St Giles' Church. The High Street was—and still is— a broad street, and in Knox's day was lined on both sides by high tenements or *lands*. The whole area was densely populated.
The house is open Monday to Saturday 10am–4.30pm. ☎ 0131 556 9579/2647. There is wheelchair access only to the ground floor of the museum and the café.

The Palace of Holyroodhouse

The Palace of Holyroodhouse began life in the early 12th century as an Augustinian monastery. Parts of the present palace date back to the 16th century. It is open daily (except 13 April, 25-26 December and during royal visits) April to October 0930–1715 hrs. November to March 0930–1545 hrs ☎ 0131 556 1096

The Museum of Scotland

Situated on Chambers Street, the museum is open Monday to Saturday 1000–1700 hrs. There is wheelchair access to the whole museum. ☎ 0131 225 7534 for further details.

The Magdalen Chapel

The Magdalen Chapel dates from 1541 and is built on the site of an earlier church dedicated to St Mary Magdalene. It is located at 41 Cowgate and is the home of the Scottish Reformation Society. The chapel is open Monday to Friday, 0930–1600 hrs. Other times by arrangement. ☎ 0131 220 1450.

Tourist Information

For the Tourist Information Centre for Edinburgh and Lothians, ☎ 0131 473 3800

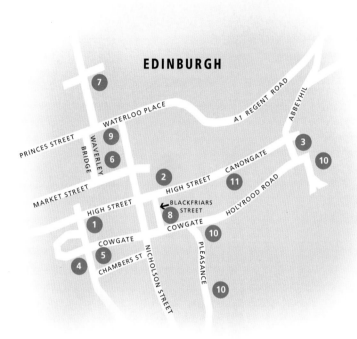

EDINBURGH

KEY TO PLACES

1 ST GILES' CATHEDRAL, HIGH STREET/ROYAL MILE

2 JOHN KNOX HOUSE, HIGH STREET/ROYAL MILE

3 PALACE OF HOLYROODHOUSE

4 MAGDALEN CHAPEL, COWGATE

5 MUSEUM OF SCOTLAND, CHAMBERS STREET

6 RAILWAY STATION, WAVERLEY BRIDGE

7 BUS STATION, ST ANDREW SQUARE

8 SITE OF CARDINAL BEATON'S HOUSE, CORNER OF BLACKFRIARS STREET AND COWGATE

9 TOURIST INFORMATION CENTRE

10 PARKING (NEAR PALACE OF HOLYROODHOUSE, ON HOLYROOD ROAD, AND ON PLEASANCE)

11 REGENT MORAY'S HOUSE, HIGH STREET/ROYAL MILE

⑧ The final years

Court intrigue, murder, assassination and threats to his own life surrounded the great reformer's closing years, but to the end he remained the bold and faithful preacher he had been from the first

On 24 July 1567, Mary, Queen of Scots, surrendered her crown to her infant son James, and a few days later, Knox preached at his coronation in the Church of the Holy Rude in Stirling. During the years of the king's minority, Scotland would be ruled by Regents, whilst the king himself, when he came of age, would reign first as James VI of Scotland and later in 1603 as James I of England Scotland and Ireland.

The series of events that led to Mary's abdication of the throne can be briefly told. Her proposed marriage to Don Carlos of Spain never took place. Instead, on 29 July 1565, she married her cousin Henry Stewart, Lord Darnley, the eldest son of Matthew, Earl of Lennox. Darnley was a few years younger than Mary; he was tall, handsome, fond of hunting and hawking, but weak, foolish and self-willed—and Mary soon began to despise him. At the same time, an Italian called David Rizzio, a skilful musician and suspected agent of the Pope, was becoming increasingly popular with the Queen. He became one of her most confidential advisers, meeting with her early and late, and receiving generous gifts from

Above: St Giles Cathedral

Facing page: Stained glass window in St Giles, depicting Knox preaching at the funeral of the Regent Moray

Top: Henry Stewart, Lord Darnley

Above: James Hepburn, Earl of Bothwell

her. Rumours abounded. Because of his considerable influence at Court, Rizzio gained enemies amongst the Protestant nobles who saw him as a threat to the nation's liberties. Darnley's jealousy was also roused by his closeness to the Queen, and the result was Rizzio's murder on 9 March 1566. A year later, in February 1567, a house in Edinburgh in which Darnley was recuperating from an illness was blown up with gunpowder. When Darnley's body was later found in the garden, it was clear that he had been strangled.

The man behind Lord Darnley's murder was James Hepburn, Earl of Bothwell. After Rizzio's death Mary's affections had been settled on him, and it was widely suspected that it was with her knowledge, consent, and aid that he had murdered her husband. At a mockery of a trial, Bothwell was acquitted of

Above: Murder of David Rizzio in the Palace of Holyroodhouse

Above: Lochleven Castle where Mary Queen of Scots was eventually imprisoned

Darnley's murder and after securing a divorce from his wife with the help of the Roman Catholic Archbishop of St Andrews, he and Mary were married. Darnley had been dead for only three months. For the Protestant nobles it was the final straw. They were appalled at the prospect of a man like Bothwell being King of Scotland and they marched out with an army to fight him at Carberry Hill near Musselburgh. But no battle took place. So many of Bothwell's supporters deserted him that he was forced to escape, first to Orkney and then to Denmark where he spent his final days imprisoned in an island keep.

The Good Regent

Queen Mary, who had been with Bothwell at Carberry Hill, had no option but to surrender to the Protestant nobles. She was taken back to Edinburgh as a prisoner and as she was led up the High Street there were jeers from the crowds and cries for her to be burnt. The question now was, what was to be done with her? If she remained Queen, she would be certain to bring Bothwell back and that would mean civil war. So the decision was taken to imprison her in Lochleven Castle and require her to surrender her crown to her infant son James. Her brief and troubled reign as Queen of Scotland was over, with authority passing for the present to her half-brother, Lord James Stewart, Earl

Above: *James Stewart, the Regent Moray*

of Moray, who was appointed Regent of the kingdom.

Regent Moray is known to history as 'The Good Regent', and it is a title well deserved. He is described by a contemporary as: 'a godly magistrate, whom God, of His eternal and heavenly providence, hath reserved to this age, to put in execution whatever He hath by His law commandeth.' The breach between Moray and Knox had by this time been fully healed, and it was a cause of great satisfaction to Knox that Scotland at last had a ruler who was wholeheartedly committed to the truths of the gospel. He trusted Moray thoroughly.

But Knox had his own concerns. At a General Assembly of the church's leaders after Mary's arrest and imprisonment, a unanimous agreement was reached that if, as believed, she was guilty of murder and adultery, she should be executed. Knox had been one of those present and had fully concurred in the judgment. He maintained that there would be no lasting peace in the land as long as Mary was alive, and although there was little support for his views, the unfolding of events once again showed how far-sighted he was. A year after her imprisonment in Lochleven Castle Mary escaped and immediately raised an army against the supporters of the Regent. It was defeated at Langside and Mary was forced to flee into England. But her imprisonment there did not bring an end to the trouble she had stirred up. A number of prominent Scots had openly identified themselves with her and continued to seek her release and restoration to the throne. One of these supporters was the Duke of Chatelherault, who had been Regent during Mary's infancy. In him Mary had a particularly powerful ally. He was the head of the Hamilton family and had returned from France as Mary's lieutenant. During Moray's regency, however, Mary's supporters were never sufficiently numerous to wage an effective civil war.

Assassination of the Regent Moray

On 23 January 1570, Scotland suffered a great calamity. The Good Regent was assassinated. As he was riding through Linlithgow, a shot rang out from a balcony above him, and it proved fatal. The deed was particularly dreadful because of the kindness Moray had previously shown to

Above: The Regent Moray's house in the Royal Mile. It is now part of Moray House Institute of Education

Below: From an old engraving, the assassination of the Regent Moray on 23 January 1570

the very man who murdered him. His name was Hamilton of Bothwellhaugh, and he was one of those who fought for Mary at Langside. Arrested, condemned, and brought out to execution for his part in that rebellion, his life was spared by the Regent and he was set free. This was how he repaid his benefactor. On the Regent's part, however, there were no regrets. As his life ebbed away he declared that nothing would ever make him repent his act of clemency.

There was widespread sorrow at the news and Knox himself was heartbroken. Not only had he lost a dear friend but he knew how great was the loss to Scotland. The day after Moray's death, Knox poured out his heart to God in his sermon in which he thanked God for a man who had brought peace and stability to the nation. The

Top: Statue of Knox inside St Giles

Above: *Sketch of John Knox's house*

Regent was buried on February 14 below the south aisle of St Giles. As Knox preached the funeral sermon on the words: 'Blessed are the dead who die in the Lord', he declared, 'He is at rest, O Lord; we are left in extreme misery'. Three thousand people were moved to tears.

Divided nation

The death of Moray led to a deepening of the country's divisions. The infant king's grandfather, the Earl of Lennox was appointed Regent the following month. But he too met a violent death. In August 1571 he was in Stirling when an attack was made on the town by the supporters of Queen Mary, and Lennox was taken prisoner; he was shot and killed as the friends who had freed him in a counter-attack tried to lead him to safety. The situation worsened during the brief regency of Lennox's successor, the Earl of Mar. One historian tells us: 'There never was a sadder time in the whole history of Scotland. There had been civil wars in previous reigns, but never had the contending sides been so cruel and merciless. When prisoners were taken, they were at once put to death. And it was not only near Edinburgh that fighting went on, but in other parts of the country.' The Regent Mar died in 1572, not violently as his two predecessors had done, but, it was said, of a broken heart because: 'he loved peace and could not have it.' But a cessation of conflict was in sight. The new Regent, the Earl of Morton, succeeded at last in securing the help of Queen

Elizabeth of England, and in the spring of 1573, the bastion of Mary's supporters, Edinburgh Castle, was finally taken and the civil war came to an end.

Knox remained in Edinburgh for as long as he could during the conflict, but with the Castle in the hands of the Queen's party, it had become a dangerous place for him. On one occasion a shot was fired through the window of his house and the musket-ball embedded itself in the ceiling—had Knox been sitting where he normally sat it would certainly have struck him. The incident brought to him a deputation of Edinburgh citizens who told him that they were resolved to defend his life, even if it should cost them their own. John knew that his departure from Edinburgh would leave his enemies free to pursue their objectives without his opposition and they would accuse him of cowardice. But the readiness of his friends to die for him persuaded John, though: 'sore against his will'.

From Edinburgh to St Andrews

Knox left Edinburgh on 5 May 1571, an ill and frail man, weary of the world, and longing for the release of death. His destination was St Andrews where he was to remain for a whole year. Here he was free from personal danger but not from involvement in controversy. In the parish church, where he had begun his public ministry, he preached a series of sermons on Daniel 11 in which he boldly denounced the crimes of the Queen's party. It gave such offence to his enemies that they

Above: The pulpit from which Knox is traditionally said to have preached in St Andrews. It stood in the parish church until the late 1700s but since then has been in St Salvator's Chapel in North Street

attempted to ruin his character by circulating a slanderous report about him. During his time in St Andrews, Knox also published *An Answer to a Letter written by James Tyrie, a Scottish Jesuit.* Tyrie had tried to convert his brother, a Protestant, back to Roman Catholicism, and this *Answer,* written at the brother's request was Knox's response.

But it was not all controversy in St Andrews. One thing that gave Knox great pleasure was to mingle with the university students. He would often exhort them to study hard, to know God, to acquaint themselves with God's work in Scotland, and to be faithful to his cause. One of these students, James Melville, afterwards minister in Anstruther, has left us a most vivid description of Knox's preaching at this time. In his diary he writes, 'Of all the benefits that I had that year [1571], was the coming of that most notable prophet and apostle of our nation, Mr John Knox, to St Andrews ... I heard him teach there the prophecies of Daniel, that summer and the winter following. I had my pen and my little book, and took away such things as I could comprehend. In the opening up of his text, he was moderate the space of half an hour; but when he entered to application, he made me so to grew [shudder] and tremble, that I could not hold a pen to write.' Melville tells us that Knox was very weak at this time and describes how he had to be supported by a servant as he made his way to the church and helped into the pulpit: 'where he behoved to lean at his first entry'. But then the weakness would pass: 'Ere he had done with his sermon, he was so active and vigorous, that he was like to ding the pulpit in blads [beat the pulpit in pieces], and fly out of it.'

Knox's last days

The weakness to which Melville refers increased to such an extent that it seemed likely that Knox would end his days in St Andrews. In the month of July 1572, however, a truce was agreed between the Regent's forces and the supporters of Queen Mary which allowed him to return to Edinburgh. A practical problem had immediately to be faced. It had been difficult enough in Knox's best days to make his voice heard in the vast St Giles' Church, but now it was impossible. So the Tolbooth Church was used instead and there he preached as often as he was able, dwelling on the theme on which he had long wished to close his ministry—the sufferings and death of Christ

One of his first appearances in the pulpit after his return took place in circumstances of great sadness. News had reached Scotland of what is known in history as the Massacre of St Bartholomew's Day of 1572 when tens of thousands of French Protestants were murdered on the

Above: Scene of George Wishart's martyrdom, St Andrews Castle

Left: Knox returning to his home after preaching his final sermon on 9 November 1572

orders of the French king, Charles XI. Summoning up his strength, Knox thundered forth the vengeance of heaven against 'that cruel murderer the king of France' and ordered Le Croc, the French ambassador, to go and tell his master that sentence was pronounced against him in Scotland, that the Divine vengeance would never depart from him or his house unless they repented.

Knox's last appearance in the pulpit was on 9 November 1572. In view of his seriously declining strength, John Lawson of Aberdeen had been chosen as a colleague, and on 9 November, Knox preached at his induction. He concluded the service with a fervent prayer for divine blessing on both minister and the congregation; and then, 'leaning upon his staff and the arm of an attendant, he crept down the street, which was lined with the audience, who, as if anxious to take the last sight of their beloved pastor, followed him until he entered his house, from which he never came out alive.'

Knowing himself that the end was approaching, Knox was anxious to meet once more with his elders. When they gathered in his room, he said to them: 'The day approaches, and is now before the door, for which I have frequently and vehemently thirsted, when I shall be released from my great labours and innumerable sorrows, and shall be with Christ. And now, God is my witness, whom I have served in the spirit in the gospel of his Son, that I have taught nothing but the true and solid doctrine of the gospel of

Above: Knox on his deathbed

Below: The exact location of Knox's grave is not known. This stone formerly marked the traditional site in Parliament Square outside St Giles. It is now located inside St Giles

the Son of God, and have had it only for my object to instruct the ignorant, to confirm the faithful, to comfort the weak, the fearful and the distressed, by the promises of grace, and to fight against the proud and rebellious by the divine threatenings.' Knox then defended his 'threatenings' saying, 'I know that many have frequently complained, and do still loudly proclaim, of my too great severity; but God knows that my mind was always void of hatred to the persons of those against whom I thundered the severest judgments. I cannot deny that I felt the greatest abhorrence at the sins in which they indulged, but still I kept this one thing in view, that, if possible, I might gain them to the Lord.'

On the afternoon of the final day of his life, 24 November 1572, he asked his wife to read to him the fifteenth chapter of Paul's first letter to the Corinthians. 'Is not that a comfortable chapter?' he asked. Later, he requested that she should read the seventeenth chapter of John's Gospel: 'Where I first cast my anchor'. Margaret also read to him from Calvin's sermons on Ephesians. As the day drew to a close he gave a deep sigh, and whispered, 'Now it is come.' Moments later, John Knox 'rendered up his spirit, apparently without pain or movement, so that he seemed rather to fall asleep than to die.'

The greatest of Scotsmen

In life Knox had enemies who did their best to destroy his character—and he has them still. His anti-Catholicism, his *First*

Blast of the Trumpet, his confrontations with Mary, Queen of Scots, his doctrinal convictions, and his decisive influence on the future direction of Scottish theology, continue to this day to make him in some eyes an object of hatred and contempt.

But the hatred and contempt are undeserved. Like all great men he undoubtedly had his faults. He could be obstinate, he was at times guilty of using intemperate language, and he did not always act wisely. Nevertheless, John Knox was a man of honour and integrity, whose chief concern in life was the glory of Christ and the Christian good of his fellow human beings. As a writer, a leader of men, and above all as a preacher of God's word, he made an outstanding contribution to the reformation of the Church. His servant Richard Bannatyne described him as: 'a man of God, the light of Scotland, the comfort of the Kirk within the same, the mirror of godliness, and a pattern and example to all true ministers in purity of life, soundness of doctrine, and boldness in reproof of wickedness.' Knox is to be remembered and honoured for these things. So too for his vision for the education of the Scottish people, his conviction that a country's rulers must be subject to the country's laws, his courage in the face of danger, his deep sympathy for the poor and oppressed, his zeal for the purity of the church, and his commitment to the theology of the Reformation.

Above: *Statue of Knox in the courtyard of New College. The inscription on the base of the statue reads: 'Erected by Scotsmen who are mindful of the benefits conferred by John Knox on their native land 1896'*

Thomas Carlyle spoke of him as: 'The most excellent man our country has produced'. And certainly, to those who whole-heartedly sympathise with the great work of his life, with the gospel that he preached, and with the principles of the reformed church he was so largely instrumental in creating, he will ever be the greatest of Scotsmen.

Above: New College, the Mound, Edinburgh

TRAVEL DETAILS

1. Stirling

For street map and for tourist and travel information on Stirling see details at the end of Chapter 6

2. Edinburgh

For street map and tourist and travel information on Edinburgh see details at the end of Chapter 7

3. Lochleven Castle

Kinross is situated 27 miles (44 kilometres) north of Edinburgh, 15 miles (24 kilometres) south of Perth. Visitors travelling by car should leave the M90 at junction 6 and follow the signposts for the castle. For details of bus services to Kinross, ☎ City Link, 08705 505050

Lochleven Castle is in the care of Historic Scotland. It is only accessible by boat. The castle is open Monday to Saturday 0930–1830 hrs. (April to September) with final sailing at 1715 hrs. and Monday to Saturday 0930–1630 hrs. (October) with final sailing at 1515 hrs. For further details, ☎ 0131 668 8600.

4. St Andrews

St Salvator's Chapel, North Street.
The chapel is normally open Monday to Friday from 0900–1700 hrs. It is closed on public holidays. To check beforehand, ☎ St Andrews University, 01334 476161.

Samuel Rutherford and Thomas Halyburton

Between St Rule's tower and the Cathedral Visitor Centre lie the graves of two great Scottish ministers, Samuel Rutherford (1600–61) and Thomas Halyburton (1674–1712). Rutherford is best known today for his letters. The inscription on his gravestone reads:
  'Here lyes the Reverend M. Samuell Rutherfoord

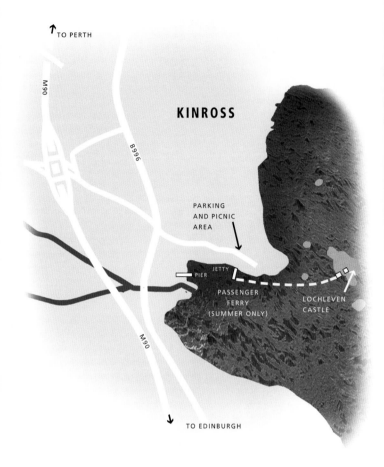

professor of Divinity in the University of St Andrews who died March the 29th

1661'. There follows a moving verse that commends his virtues.

Thomas Halyburton was buried beside Rutherford at his own request. The inscription on his gravestone reads: "Here lies the body of Thomas Halyburton, minister of the Gospel. He was born at Dublin Dec. 25th 1674, and ordained minister of Ceres May 1st 1700. In April 1710 he was

admitted Professor of Divinity in the New College, St Andrews, and on Sept. 25th 1712 at seven in the morning he fell asleep in Jesus".

For street map and for other tourist and travel information on St Andrews see details at the end of Chapters 1 and 2.

KEY TO PLACES

- **A** ST ANDREWS
- **H** HADDINGTON
- **B** BERWICK UPON TWEED
- **D** DOLLAR AND CASTLE CAMPBELL
- **S** STERLING
- **K** KINROSS AND LOCHLEVEN CASTLE

GLASGOW

EDINBURGH

NEWCASTLE

LONDONDERRY

BELFAST

DUBLIN

LIVERPOOL

MANCHESTER

M62

M56

M6

BIRMINGHAM

M1

M40

M5

M4

M25

LONDON

M3

M25

M26

M6

UNITED KINGDOM AND EIRE

TRAVEL NOTES

USEFUL INFORMATION

The following notes are for those who are new to visiting places of interest, and especially for overseas visitors; a little information about your host country will make you feel more at home and less of a stranger.

1 What do you wear?
Travelling on public transport can be hot and dirty; so it is better to dress comfortably rather than smartly – especially footwear. Wear thin layers topped with a light waterproof that can protect from wind as well as rain. It is easier to carry two or more thinner garments than a heavy coat and jumper. Remember that the only reliable thing about the British weather is that it is unreliable.

2 Take great care with personal belongings. Keep wallets and purses out of sight on your person – bags can easily be snatched. Cameras and other personal items should be kept secure at all times. A rucksack may be good for your back, but in crowds it can be opened and items removed without your

knowledge. Never put a bag down and walk off, it is a security hazard and will probably have disappeared when you return. Don't assume that your property is more secure because you are in the heart of rural Britain.

*For overseas visitors.
Do not carry your passport with you, unless you plan to change money. Hotels have a safe where you can store valuables. Carry a photocopy of the relevant pages of your passport; if the original is lost then it will be easier for your embassy to issue a temporary document.

3 Obtain a map of public transport in the area you are travelling. Basic maps are free from tourist information kiosks; bus and railway maps are available from bus and railway stations.

4 Always respect the places you visit. Take note of 'No Entry' and 'Private' signs. A private dwelling may once have had a connection with the subject of this book, but please do not disturb the present residents. Usually there will be an indication at the property if it is open for public viewing.

5 Photography. Respect any 'Photography not permitted' signs. In some museums and historic buildings you may take photographs, but you are not permitted to use a tripod since this can be very annoying to other visitors. Bear this in mind when deciding on the speed of film you buy. You may be able to use a monopod, but always enquire first to save hassle. You are well advised not to buy film from a street vendor, however cheap it may appear; old or

poor quality film can ruin your valuable memories. Always buy film or Flash cards in a reputable shop, and always keep the receipt.

6 In a museum, exhibition or church

do not touch anything that you are not permitted to handle. Not only can an object be damaged, but also in certain circumstances prosecution may result.

7 Respect graves in a cemetery, church or churchyard. Please be careful not to cause offence, especially if a service is taking place or if someone is sitting quietly by a grave.

8 When walking in the countryside

please respect the country code. Leave gates as you found them – whether open or closed. Keep to the paths,

or walk around the edge of fields. Do not drop litter – farm animals are not smart and will chew on your discarded litter, often with tragic results. If you have a dog with you, ensure that it does not worry any livestock. Never light a fire.

9 Litter. Please be careful with the disposal of all litter including gum. Reference libraries and museums may ask you to

remove gum if they see you chewing.

10 You will probably find it useful to put together a tourist pack. We suggest the following: a notebook, a pen or pencil, a small torch with batteries that work and a small medical kit.

11 Eating out. For most trips you may prefer to take a packed lunch. City eating places can be expensive. If a hot meal is required there are many different types of food outlets to suit all tastes and styles. Many Garden Centres have excellent cafeterias or restaurants and are usually good value for money. These

The British Museum

are normally open for food between 1000 and 1600 hours. Good rural public houses can also provide quality service.

12 Disabled visitors.

All public buildings in the UK are under a legal requirement to be wheelchair accessible; those in charge of such places are usually very helpful, but in old buildings full access is not always possible.

13 Public conveniences (restrooms).

In cities these are usually open until about 1800 hours. Most major stores, large petrol (gas) stations, restaurants or cafés

will have conveniences. Always carry tissues with you, as some public conveniences will not provide toilet tissue.

14 Especially for London

Because of the Congestion Charge and the difficulty of parking, we strongly advise you against taking a car into the centre of London.

The Congestion Charge

The congestion charge is £5 daily in 2003. The aim is to reduce traffic, making journeys and delivery times more reliable, and raise millions each week to re-

invest in London's transport system.

Who has to pay the charge?

There are some exemptions and discounts, but if you are due to pay and do not, a Penalty Charge Notice will be issued.

This website tells you about central London congestion charging and what you need to do.

Website: www.cclondon.com

Transport maps

A London combined network map—bus, underground (tube) and overland railway—is available from bus garages and railway stations; also many newsagents who display the London transport sign.

Travel to all London sites will be referred to from one of the main London termini. The best time to travel into London on a weekday is after 0930 hours. You can save money if your train leaves after this time, and you avoid the rush hour. The transport companies have divided London into zones, and the number of zones visited will determine the cost of the ticket. The best ticket to buy is a Travel Card (you can get daily, weekly or monthly cards) which will enable you to go by train, tube and bus all on the same ticket. Make sure that you buy the right ticket for the places to be visited; just ask the clerk in the ticket office.

If you are thinking of using **Buses in central London,** remember to buy your ticket before you travel. If you do not have a Travel Card which includes your bus fare, it will be necessary to buy a ticket from one of the **ticket machines which are at all central London bus stops.**

The ticket machines are very simple to use and sell Adult and Child single tickets as well as One Day Bus Passes

You'll need the exact money (as they don't give change) They take £2, £1, 50p, 20p, 10p and 5p coins.

A guide to using buses if you have a disability

An increasing number of low floor accessible buses are being introduced to London and currently run on more than 35 routes across the capital. They have a low flat floor to make travel easier for the elderly and disabled customers as well as those with pushchairs. For further information on routes, prices and frequency of tubes and buses in London, call 020 7222 1234

Refreshments in London

are many and various. It would be best to have a packed lunch as we suggest above, but if you prefer hot food, please take note of the following: Always check that the food and drink prices are listed before you place an order. Always query any discrepancies before payment is made. Drinks and food from road-side vendors in the cities will be more expensive.

Unless you have a good budget, the best places for light refreshments are fast food restaurants, especially if you just want a hot drink. Another possibility worth investigating is any café that builders are using! They may not be the most luxurious, but the workers normally know where to find good wholesome food, that it is served quickly and hot – and at a reasonable price.

MONARCHS AND REGENTS

Scottish Monarchs

James V: 1513–1542

Mary I (Mary, Queen of Scots): 1542–1567

James VI 1567–1625 (from 1603 as James I of England
Scotland and Ireland)

Scottish Regents

Earl of Arran: 1543–1554

Mary of Lorraine (Mary of Guise)—Queen Regent:
1554–1559

From 1559–1561 Scotland was governed by a council
and then by Parliament until Mary, Queen of Scots (who
had been queen since her birth in 1542) arrived in
Scotland. She surrendered her crown to her infant son
James in 1567

Earl of Moray: 1567–1570

Earl of Lennox: 1570–1571

Earl of Mar: 1571–1572

Earl of Morton: 1572–1578

Edward VI

English Monarchs

Henry VIII: 1509–1547

Edward VI: 1547–1553

Mary Tudor (Bloody Mary): 1553–1558

Elizabeth I: 1558–1603

Mary Tudor

BIBLIOGRAPHY

John Knox, *History of the Reformation
in Scotland,* Banner of Truth

Elizabeth Whitley, *Plain Mr Knox,*
Christian Focus Publications

Thomas M'Crie, *John Knox,* Free
Presbyterian Publications

THE AUTHOR

After finishing his studies at the Free
Church of Scotland College in Edinburgh
in 1987, David Campbell was Minister of
Geneva Road Evangelical Baptist Church,
Darlington until 2002 when he accepted
a call to be Senior Pastor of Grace Baptist
Church, Carlisle, Pennsylvania. He is
married to Mairi and they have two
children, Megan and Caitriona.

c.1514	John Knox is born in Giffordgate, Haddington.
February 1528	Martyrdom of Patrick Hamilton in St Andrews.
December 1542	James V of Scotland dies and is succeeded by his daughter Mary I [Mary, Queen of Scots] who becomes Queen at the age of one week.
January 1543	Earl of Arran appointed Regent of Scotland
c.1543	Knox becomes tutor to the sons of Hugh Douglas of Longniddry and John Cockburn of Ormiston.
March 1546	Martyrdom of George Wishart in St Andrews.
May 1546	Cardinal Beaton murdered in St Andrews Castle.
January 1547	Henry VIII of England dies and is succeeded by his young son Edward VI.
April 1547	Knox enters St Andrews Castle.
May 1547	He is called to be a preacher.
July 1547–January 1549	A prisoner on a French galley.
January 1549	He is released and returns to England.
April 1549	Appointed a preacher in Berwick-upon-Tweed.
Summer 1551	Appointed a preacher in St Nicholas' Church, Newcastle.
December 1551	In addition to his duties in Newcastle, Knox is appointed a chaplain to King Edward VI.
April 1553	Knox leaves Newcastle for London and spends several months as an itinerant preacher in the south of England.
July 1553	King Edward VI of England dies and his sister Mary Tudor is proclaimed Queen.
January 1554	Knox leaves England for the continent to escape the persecution of Protestants by Queen Mary.
April 1554	Mary of Lorraine, mother of Mary, Queen of Scots, becomes Regent of Scotland
November 1554	After visiting several places in Switzerland, Knox is appointed one of the ministers of a congregation of English refugees in Frankfurt.
March 1555	He leaves Frankfurt for Geneva.
Autumn 1555	Returns to Scotland and preaches in many different places.
July 1556	Returns to Geneva as one of the ministers of the English congregation there.

Autumn 1557–	Knox in Dieppe in connection with a possible return to Scotland.
Spring 1558	He returns to Geneva and publishes his notorious *First Blast of the Trumpet*.
November 1558	Queen Mary Tudor dies enabling the Protestant refugees to return home. She is succeeded by her half-sister Elizabeth I.
January 1559	Knox leaves Geneva for Dieppe.
May 1559	He arrives in Leith.
July 1559	Appointed minister of St Giles in Edinburgh.
October 1559	Mary of Lorraine suspended from the Regency.
June 1560	Mary of Lorraine dies.
July 1560	Treaty of Edinburgh signed by which all French and English troops to leave Scotland.
August 1560	Scottish parliament abolishes the jurisdiction of the Pope in Scotland and prohibits the celebrating of the Roman Catholic mass.
December 1560	Knox's first wife, Marjory, dies.
August 1561	Mary, Queen of Scots arrives in Scotland.
March 1564	Knox marries Margaret Stewart.
July 1567	Mary, Queen of Scots, surrenders her throne to her infant son James [James VI of Scotland and James I of England]. Her half brother, James Stewart, Earl of Moray, is appointed Regent.
January 1570	Regent Moray is assassinated and is succeeded by the Earl of Lennox.
May 1571	Knox, for his safety, forced to leave Edinburgh for St Andrews.
August 1571	Regent Lennox dies and is succeeded by the Earl of Mar.
July 1572	Knox returns to Edinburgh.
October 1572	Regent Mar dies and is succeeded by the Earl of Morton.
9 November 1572	Knox preaches his final sermon.
24 November 1572	John Knox dies in his home in Edinburgh at the age of 58.

Meet John Bunyan

Above: John Bunyan. From a copy of a portrait in the National Portrait Gallery, London, by Thomas Sadler

Top: Elstow Green and Moot Hall (early 16th century)

'John, there's a warrant out for your arrest, you know! Perhaps we should cancel the meeting?' The defiant preacher responded, 'We need not be ashamed to preach—it is God's word!' There was a hush as John Bunyan commenced to pray, but hardly had he begun when, without warning, the village constable burst into the room of the isolated farmhouse. The gathering was thrown into confusion and many of the hearers became alarmed and fearful of what would happen next. Calmly the tall, red-haired preacher spoke a few words of encouragement to his small country congregation before being led away.

John Bunyan was under arrest for daring to preach the gospel in a Bedfordshire village!

During the middle years of the 17th century, England saw many

Above: "The Jetty," Elstow High Street. In Bunyan's time this was a dropping off-point for the London–Bedford horse-drawn stage coach

next twelve years in Bedford Gaol because of his beliefs.

Born into a poor Bedfordshire family, Bunyan grew up as an idle lad, known locally for his lying and cursing; yet he was to become a world famous figure even in his own lifetime. Though barely literate, he would eventually pen what is still today probably one of the best-known classic titles ever to be written—*The Pilgrim's Progress*.

Many have written on the life, times and theology of this 17th century writer, preacher, and prisoner of faith and conscience. This book presents the story of Bunyan together with tourist details and information connected with Bedfordshire's famous son, who became widely known as 'the tinker from Elstow'.

Travel with John Bunyan

JOHN PESTELL
ILLUSTRATED 128 PAGES
£9.99
1 903087 12 0

who made a stand for freedom of conscience to worship outside of the Church of England. Following the civil war that had divided the nation for nine long years, they were imprisoned without a proper trial or hearing for their faith and conviction as the new monarch, Charles II, peevishly tried to restore the rule of law across the realm.

John Bunyan was arrested and sent to prison for preaching without a licence from the Church of England. He would spend the

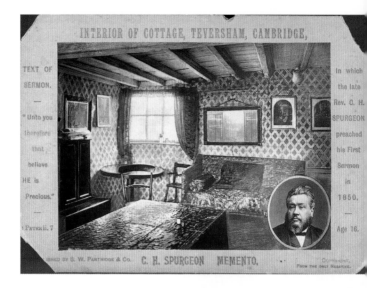

Meet CH Spurgeon

Top: The only known photograph of the interior of Spurgeon's cottage in Teversham

Above: Job Spurgeon was imprisoned twice in Chelmsford jail for preaching without a licence in his home town of Dedham in Essex

Susannah could not believe her eyes—the rumours about him being an uncouth country bumpkin seemed all too true. His clothes looked as though a village tailor had cut them out in the dark, and around his neck he wore a large piece of black satin that had seen better days. Worse was to come: as he spoke, he waved in the air a ghastly blue handkerchief with white spots on it. If it were not so serious Susannah would have laughed out loud.

Yet after a few months this 'wild' young preacher from East Anglia was the minister of her famous London church, and just three years later Susannah married him!

Together they started and

*Above: Lavenham—a medieval delight **Right:** Charles was twenty when he met Susannah Thompson—later to become his wife*

financed the distribution of Christian books, new churches, a pastors' training college, orphanages, and almshouses.

As minister of the largest church in London, which each week attracted six thousand people to both services, his name became a household word right across the British Empire.

Every Thursday, newsagents in shops and on street corners around the world sold the script of one of his sermons. Altogether between 1855 and his death in 1892, one hundred and eight million copies of these sermons were sold at a penny each. He wrote over one hundred and fifty books; and one hundred and ten years after his death they are still widely read.

Charles Haddon Spurgeon was a friend and confidant to Prime Ministers as well as the ordinary people. Rumour had it that Queen Victoria came in disguise to hear him. He has been called 'The Prince of Preachers' but he was more, much more.

Travel with CH Spurgeon

CLIVE ANDERSON
ILLUSTRATED 128 PAGES
£9.99   1 903087 11 2

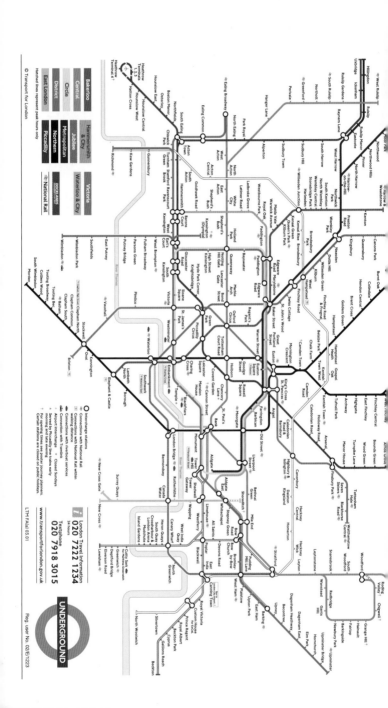